This entire book is all of one sentence:
On that day, God will be one, and His name one.

What is it that breathes fire into the equations and makes a universe for them to describe? The usual approach of science of constructing a mathematical model cannot answer the questions of why there should be a universe for the model to describe. Why does the universe go to all the bother of existing?

(Dr. Stephen W. Hawking's *A Brief History of Time: From the Big Bang to Black Holes*, "Conclusion" chapter 11, p.184).

[I]f we do discover a complete theory, it should in time be understandable in broad principle by everyone, not just a few scientists. Then we shall all, philosophers, scientists, and just ordinary people, be able to take part in the discussion of the question of why it is that we and the universe exist. If we find the answer to that, it would be the ultimate triumph of human reason

(ibid p.185).

It was a beautiful Galilean, blue-sky day. Though in my own spiritual island-bubble, I was just strolling aimlessly at that point by the shore that's a beeline down from the shrine of the great Tanna, Rabbi Meir Baal HaNess. This was the very place where the late Kabbalist Rabbi Yitzhak Kaduri used to come to toivel, saying this is where Miriam's Well came to its final resting spot. The water of the Kinneret was like a sheet of little mirrors reflecting the sun's light.

And then it caught me.

At first it appeared as merely another little mirror reflecting off the water. But then it got brighter, and then stood out distinctly, almost winking at me, as it approached the shore. Its beacon became so directed at me, I could no longer even try to ignore it. I somehow just knew that it was meant for me personally, beckoning me to fish it out.

So I did.

I plucked it from the water. It was a bottle sealed with one of those hermetic but reseal-able plugs. I twisted off the cap, and a note popped up, like a tissue. I tried to pull it out, but the note unfolded while its bottom corner held fast, remaining immovable. Amazing, I thought. I looked down to read:

> *The sea of Torah is vast.*
> *The world was created with a distinct purpose.*
> *There isn't even one extraneous person on earth.*
> *You cannot stroll aimlessly.*
> *You must find your direction, function, and mission*
> *and begin. Pursue it.*

Then that note popped back inside the bottle and another note corner peeked up. It read:

> *Don't wait – get busy already!*

And then a third:

> *And God will be king over all the earth:*
> *on that day God will be [acknowledged] one,*
> *and His name be one (Zechariah 14:9).*

Then I heard their discussion. Two familiar folk.

They asked each other questions, but were unable to answer their own questions.

Then I felt myself drifting, lighting out in their direction, seemingly to the middle of nowhere, pulled merely by their discussion, to meet up with them, because their questions remained unanswered.

[O]ur goal is a complete *understanding* of the events around us, and of our own existence

(Ibid, last lines of chapter 10 "The Unification of Physics", p.179).

The whole history of science has been the gradual realization that events do not happen in an arbitrary manner, but that they reflect a certain underlying order

(ibid, chapter 8, p. 129).

Torah for the sake of teaching it, [meaning] active Torah, is beyond the angels' experience

(Aryeh Carmell's Strive For Truth
(translation of Rabbi Eliyahu Dessler's
Michtav MeEliyahu, Letter From Eliyahu),
part 5, parashat "*Yitro*" p. 213.)

DISILLUSIONS:

A Spiritual GPS For the Journeyer
&
The Real New World Order

Yemima Bakol

Published by
Targum Publishers
Shlomo ben Yosef 131a/1
Jerusalem 93805
editor@targumpublishers.com

B"H

In the name of God, we will do and we will succeed.

*

This book is dedicated
to
The Holy One Blessed Be He

to
Rabbi Moshe Chaim Armoni shlit"a
especially for his book Bati L'Armoni on the parsha

to
Benny Azulai (from Yaffe Nof Beit Hakerem)
who introduced me to the writings of Richard Bach,
then did teshuva, and disappeared

and
to
Mr. Akiva Atwood
for liking and publishing my work – I'm grateful!

*

ON

CHAPTER ONE

Mind if I join you guys?" I asked as my bike finally came to a stop. By today they had at least gone to using their Hebrew names: Aryeh Lieb (literally, Lion Heart) and Dan Shimon (named after the two tribes) were lying on the grass in the clearing of a hay field in mid-west USA. It was a beautiful late summer afternoon, with a nice feeling of calm.

They looked up not in the least surprised. Must have thought I was coming to hop a 10-minute flight. Carried over from their Illusions, they continued into their Disillusions to fly $3 rides.[1]

"Not at all. Pull up a seat," Aryeh Lieb said in a friendly tone, waving his hand in mock-formality to a bald patch on the ground near the two.

"I couldn't help getting a whiff of the interesting conversation going on here," I said. The two jerked their heads suddenly and slightly sat up more, unable to hide their puzzled surprise and curiosity. You could almost hear their thoughts: 'How did this guy know or hear what we were talking about, sitting here in the middle of nowhere?!'

I didn't really mean to ruffle them right off the bat, and I tried to return the laid-back feeling. "Sorry to disappoint you if you thought I came to fly," I said.

"That's okay," Dan Shimon reassured me, but still looked as if

---

1 *Illusions: The Adventures of a Reluctant Messiah* by Richard Bach.

he were waiting for a good answer, any explanation from me.

There was a light gust of wind that sent the tall grass not that far from us in a synchronized line dance. Dan Shimon's long black hair was also blown back a bit from his face from the breeze, though it didn't help to relax him any, now after my remark.

I had initially decided to hold my tongue. Mind my own business. But then, after more than 30 years, it occurred to me that…this IS my business. That I am, in the most literal of manners and meanings, minding my own business. Thus, I resolved to butt into their convo.

Just then a young couple pulled up in a new sports car. Maybe newlyweds. They wanted to be able to fly together. So there was no question. Aryeh Lieb's Fleet could only take one passenger. My odd-ball mountain bike was not, and obviously could not just slide into the barnstorming business. Dan Shimon, with his Travel Air for three, happily got to his feet to offer service.

Once they were off the ground, I looked at Aryeh Lieb and, as I looked up at the small plane and pointed, I commented, "You know, not everything is so up in the air." He gave me a half-smile and looked at me humorously, enjoying the pun. Then his smile vanished. He realized that the simple sentence reflected something much deeper than appeared. Maybe something that would shake up or even shatter the lessons learned to-date.

I looked up and breathed deeply, spreading my arms to either side, "Ahh. Glorious Big-Sky Country." Aryeh Lieb was still eyeing me, waiting for me to explain myself.

"If you look at the sky over there," I started, pointing up toward the east, "it looks like the same sky as over there," I continued, waving my extended index finger over to the west.

"I don't know much about flying. Every time I've ever flown, I was e pluribus unum in Economy Class. Preferably in an aisle seat." He flashed a full smile with a light chuckle. Good, I thought. I definitely do not mean to be threatening. I really wanted to keep it as relaxed and friendly as it had been.

"As you fly up there, and I mean from where you sit in the cockpit, your gauges don't register 'east' and then 'west' as you fly by, do they?" He nodded. "It's all sky. There are no lines or signs up there indicating that this is east or differentiating the precise moment you go from east to south. Right?" He nodded again.

"Normally, this wouldn't really matter. But, imagine you were flying near an enemy country. You would have it marked on your maps and computerized in your flight gear. But the sky itself doesn't mark a border." Once again he nodded, eyes off to the side as his head was bent slightly down, concentrating on following my line of thinking.

"The sky everywhere looks the same," I continued.

"Maybe that's actually part of the illusion," he picked up, trying to suggest the meaning of my words. "It looks alike, but if you fly, even accidentally, into their air space, you're in big trouble, to put it lightly."

"So basically what you're saying is that your life depends on whoever it was that programmed your flight instruments and whoever it was that 'did' your maps. You rely on the knowledge and accuracy those guys had in providing you direction," I came to my "sub-conclusion".

He raised his left eyebrow slightly. "I guess you could say that," he agreed. The prospect was definitely frightening.

"Now," I continued leaning slightly forward, "what would happen if your gear and maps were, say...just slightly off?" It was more a rhetorical question.

"Slightly off," he tested. "Slightly" pause "off," he tested the words again and let his voice carry a bit on the second word. He wasn't ready to take answering just yet. Aryeh Lieb needed time now to swallow what I was hinting at.

The bomb fell. It was getting across. This had humongous implications: About everything he had ever learned. About his present teacher. We were both silent.

Just then, out of the silence, we heard the old familiar buzz.

Looking up we saw the Travel Air just come into sight. And we continued to watch in silence as Dan Shimon spiraled down for the happy couple and then finally landed, in yet another of his typically supernatural, yet undetected-so, landings, snug and smug next to Aryeh Lieb's Fleet.

The young couple then wanted to take a couple pictures. Dan Shimon completed his perfect service with a smile and a wave, "Now you folks have a good one." And they were on their way. They were barely a yard or so out of their parking spot and he plopped down next to us in the clearing.

"Miss anything interesting?" Dan Shimon asked humorously.

"How about if I toss you in the deep end, but then help you to swim?" I replied. He smiled enjoying the sudden challenge. "Dan Shimon," I got straight to the point, "in one of your alternate, parallel lives, you get murdered by a guy with a shotgun."

"Yeah, I remember that," Aryeh Lieb sighed.

"Wait a minute," Dan Shimon tried to get things straight. "Did you read his 1977 book or not?"

"Of course," I retorted. "That's just one of the items I'd like to change." They looked surprised and puzzled. "Anyway, how could I forget such a book? It was probably the only published document in the history of civilization that ended in a nonconformistic COMMA!"

"Hey, forget that," Dan Shimon added. "What about the fact that it begins all gooked up with fingerprints all full of aircraft grease?!" It gave me the feeling he was now on my side. We all smiled at that. "But it was time," he went on, "and I even already wanted to get, as I put it then, 'beyond times and spaces.' You disagree?"

"Not necessarily. Maybe it was your time to go. But it didn't have to be that way. In fact, maybe you didn't have to go at all," I said.

"Should it matter?" he asked.

"Of course," I replied. "Everything matters." He gave me a look not sure how to take what I just said. "Forget for a moment your ideas of fun incorporated into the whole dramatic and gory scene. Murder in the first degree," I asked, "Is it good or bad?"

"It was done that way for a purpose. We explained that back then," they answered me together.

"Is anything really good or evil? Think about it," Dan Shimon tested me. But I surprised him.

"Yes. Definitely," I said emphatically. "But to get the full picture and understanding, let's lay things out properly. So I won't completely answer you just yet."

"Well, you've got all the time in the world to lay things out," Aryeh Lieb punned as he stretched out on the grass. And I implicitly excused myself into a virtual bubble without actually, physically, stepping away. I took an apple out of my backpack, held it in my right hand, blessed, then took a bite.

THAT

Chapter Two

Night falls quick and heavy out in the boonies. No street lights. No streets close by, for that matter, unless you count a single dirt path. No telephones or cellphones. No TV. Absolutely nothing electronic. No music playing anywhere or even a faint screech from a passing car. Pitch darkness. Absolute silence.

The one airman was stoking the campfire just set up, while the other was tending to his notorious pan-bread. "You know," I began, "this whole scene here is a perfect portrayal of life 4000 years ago."

"Now why would we need to get a feel for life 4000 years ago?" Aryeh Lieb asked.

"Because it was 4000 years ago, give or take a few years in either direction, that true understanding descended to earth." The two looked at me. "They say Abraham was three years old when he first discovered the Creator. Can you imagine – the son of the head honcho idol distributor of the entire region where he lived. Didn't you once say something like the truth can never be measured by the size of its following?"

"Something like that."

"Well, here we're talking absolutely zero following. Abraham was all by his lonesome self in what he believed and knew. One and only in all of humankind. In fact, they say Abraham was able to serve the Creator just by keeping it in his mind that he, Abraham, was the only one in the whole wide world.[2] He didn't pay heed to absolutely anyone else, because he knew for certain that he had the truth. There's a lot to learn from that."

The two fliers looked a little apprehensive. I felt one of those split-second flashes. I wasn't sure exactly where I stood, or rather where they stood, where they were holding spiritually. They have this spark and interest with all their questions, so I knew I had to proceed. I decided to just roll with it, let it flow and take all of us together on the journey and course it needed to go. And I felt thankful that I picked up on this in time.

"Now, folks, kindly scrap all notions and impressions of so-called 'preaching' or even 'religious institutions,'" I quickly instructed. Relief became apparent on their faces. "Forget anything that has to do with buildings and membership dues," I continued. "Picture in your mind how it must have looked 4000 years ago. Come on, give it a shot."

"Okay. Hmmm...Camels," Dan Shimon blurted out.

"Good," I encouraged.

"Guys in sandals walking across sand dunes," Aryeh Lieb also started to get into it.

"Figurines of various sizes and shapes, of wood and stone, scattered throughout each household," Dan Shimon chimed in, trying to actually see himself back then in the picture.

"Every natural physical phenomenon worshipped as a separate god – the sun, the moon, lightning, thunder, fire. There must have been a mix of fear and awe from everything around them. Once the sun exits the horizon, who's to say and promise it'll return tomorrow?" Aryeh Lieb added.

"Good," I picked up where I had left off. "Then comes Abraham, and opens the flaps on all four sides of his tent to welcome passers-by from every direction. 'Please come in,' he would welcome

---

2   "*HaShmata*" page between parts 1 and 2 of *Likutei Moharan* (*The Writings of Rebbe Nachman of Breslev*): "Echad haya Avraham."

them, 'and have something to eat and drink.' Don't forget that we're talking about the generation of Sodom and Gomorrah," I emphasized. Dan Shimon and Aryeh Lieb sort of jumped with their new perspective of the imagery session.

"We're talking about a guy who let in total strangers and happily fed them for free, at the very time that hospitality was, in the most literal sense, legislated illegal in neighboring Sodom and Gomorrah," I reinforced. "This is the guy who invented the word 'revolutionary'."

Aryeh Lieb quickly sat up, "Pan-bread, my fellow wayfarers?"

"You're a natural second Abraham, Aryeh Lieb," Dan Shimon pitched in. "Except for your pan-bread. Now just how inhospitable could you be?!" he concluded, giving us a little comic break and we all laughed.

"Are you two done bickering yet?" I chimed in with a smirk. "You must have been an ole husband and wife team in a past life." They shot harsh glances at each other, but with a smile, as if to say, "Hey, maybe!" then laughed again. The fire was spitting sparks and dwindling down to a mysterious glow. We considered the funny idea and the fire for a quiet moment.

"A wanderer would approach on his camel," I resumed softly. "Hot, tired and famished and see all the doors open on this house. Absolutely something unheard of then. Then he'd hear someone call him, 'Come, my friend, come have something to drink. It's really hot. You need at least to drink something. Maybe have a bite to eat too.'

"The camel-rider would pick up the cup and be just about to take that most wonderful of all – the first sip. But then Abraham would jump, 'Hey, you can't just take that. It belongs to the Creator!' Half dehydrated and totally puzzled, the former would try to figure out the sudden change in tone of hospitality.

'The what? The who?' He'd be totally stumped.

'Why, haven't you heard?' the one-man 'show' Abraham would retort in disbelief. 'There's a single Creator of all of existence. One, united, alone, absolute. Everything is His. He owns everything, and He is everything. He created all that exists and He is an expression of everything there is. And your cup and the water in it too – they're His, just as it's actually He Himself expressed through the forms of water and cup. But if you bless Him and say thanks, He allows you to drink.'

'Huh?' the thirsty Canaanite would stammer.

'Bless and it's yours. Cheers!'

'And if I don't,' he would ask with the last of his breath.

'Well then, by drinking you'd be stealing,' Abraham would say resolute.

So the former would bless, and then drink, and then drink yet a couple more refills before asking, 'What did you mean when you said the cup is part of this Creator you talk of? And do you really think He heard me?'

'Of course,' the Patriarch would assure. 'You must think He's way up on some throne high up in the heavens. No. Well, that too. But He's everywhere. He's here with us, by us, and among us right now, this very minute, and always.' The poor thirst-quenched traveler would almost pass out. No one had ever heard talk anything even close to this back then."

Just then, in the midst of our intense imagery exercise, I could see that Aryeh Lieb was taking interest in the bottle that I brought with me, or, rather, that found me. I assume that since I had it near me, he thought it might shed light on our topic. Still looking at me and listening, he motioned, asking if he could reach for it, I guessed hoping to see if the bottle had anything to say about all this. I nodded, and he quickly figured out how it worked when the corner of a little note popped up. He reluctantly pulled gently and it opened up like an unfolding flower. I leaned over to peer in and see what came up.

> *Beware of the man whose god is in the skies.*
> *George Bernard Shaw*

I decided to just go on. "Abraham would say, 'The Creator fills all of His creation, being all of existence, with Himself'." And Abraham would continue to explain as he would help his guest into a more comfortable seat. 'The cup is actually part of the Creator – it's Him expressing Himself, fulfilling a need in His world by "enclothing" Himself, as it were, by that physical thing.

'It looks like just a cup. But it's not. Nothing exists or happens on its own. That's just one of the many expressions of the Creator. That's the illusion. Don't let the illusion fool you. All things – trees, and animals, and people and things, even the air we breathe and the water we drink. That's the real illusion: to think there's anything that's anything but the Creator,' I concluded my "show".

"So the world is an illusion?" Aryeh Lieb asked, breaking us back into our here and now.

"No," I answered. "This world is very real, not an illusion. It's the appearance of everything in this world that's an illusion. We might say 'this' is a rock," I continued, pointing to a big rock just next to us. "It's not. It's the Creator expressed through the inanimate. My arm is alive and moveable because He is in it.

"If I get nabbed by a thorn as I walk by, it's not the thorn – it's Him nabbing me by means of the thorn. To think otherwise is to be caught in the sinister web of the illusion. And so, when we realize this, we won't get angry at the thorn if it nabs us, because it's just the messenger." Silence. Minds being stretched like rubber bands need time to absorb the stretch.

"Well," Dan Shimon began after thinking for a good long while, "if I'm not supposed to get mad at the messenger, then why get mad at the guy who came with the shot gun? He's just the messenger."

"I never said you should get mad at all. As far as the outcome is concerned, yes, he was the messenger. But whether or not it was right, whether or not it was good, then no. It was not good or right to do. People, unlike things and animals, have free choice. And that guy chose wrong and caused a tremendous imbalance of energy in the universe by his negative action. We'll have to discuss this at some stage, because it's an important issue. In short, Dan Shimon, our job here is to instill balance, equilibrium and good, and of course to correct imbalances caused previously. But messengers of evil in the end get prosecuted either by the courts down here on earth or those up above."

We then sat quietly contemplating the scenery, the expansive sky over the nearby field, and our thoughts. The wind whistled through the grass and never allowed silence to fully overtake us.

"I still want to know what you meant by 'off slightly,'" Aryeh Lieb stated, relying on my memory of our earlier remarks. But Dan Shimon had not been present and stood there with knitted brows and a transparent, figurative question mark all over his face.

"Actually," I began, "our entire world is slightly off. All of it."

"Tell me about it," Aryeh Lieb said. "I'm telling you, looking at how complicated and messed up everything is in the world. Sometimes I think we just need to scrap everything – wipe it all clean, tear it all down, and totally start over. Build it up again, but build it up right."

"That sounds horrible," Dan Shimon blurted incredulous.

"It is, though. I'm telling you, the whole system, in every area is so messed up and corrupted. There isn't a single area of life that hasn't been corrupted. Did you know, for example, that approximately 93% of the land for housing in Israel is held by the state – too befitting a totalitarian regime. And what about the Israeli banking too: yet another expression of absolutism and totalitarianism. Not too long ago, I went to the bank to take out some money from my own checking account and the teller got annoyed and asked me why I need to take out so much money. And yet another time I deposited an out-of-state check and the bank here tells me I can only get my money in 40 days, though it cleared AS IT'S SUPPOSED TO in two days. I mean, forget the lousy service they give you; here we are in the midst of the digital age and automatic, instant everything, and –"

"Okay, pipe down. Yes, in general there's an exagerated over-taxation –"

"It's land property and a whopping outrageously-peasant-robbing, outlandishly-poverty-keeping, horrifically- astronomical 18% sales tax and –"

"Guys, we've sort of gotten slightly off again. Remember? And I'm on your side anyway. Plus, I see you forgot where you are right now."

"Right," he was still winding down. "And then play with semantics and call it 'democracy,'" he said under his breath, finishing his rage. "It just gets all of us so frazzled."

"I totally agree. But getting back to our initial point and your question about everything being off."

"Things are way way off in this world."

"I want to discuss this," I tried to answer calmly. Dan Shimon spun around to find my bottle. They were somewhat intrigued by it, but not too much, as they were used to miracles from their Illusions. A note was poking up, so they pulled it.

> *Wikipeidia on "Grand theft defined":*
> *Generally, in the United States it is defined as*
> *intentional taking of property of others in an amount*
> *exceeding the state statutory amount.*

"So this thing has a sense of humor too, does it?!"

"What's so funny about grand theft?"

"No. Don't you get the irony? It's grand theft here, but it's authorized BY the state statutory. And that is what is hysterically oxymoronically ironic and funny." The two gave sidelong glances back at the note and with lips pursed to emphasize their mixed feelings of sarcasm and ire.

Then another note surfaced. After one of them pulled, the following note unfurled –

*

> *And also the bed needs to be adjusted slightly from the place its standing;*
> *and also the table too needs to be slightly adjusted from its place;*
> *and also the menorah too needs to be slightly adjusted from its place...*
> *to put them in proper order...*
> *and took the rose from below...*

They both looked hard at it and furrowed their brows yet again.

"Can't make heads or tails of this one," one said.

"I'm stumped," said the other.

"Listen," I began slowly. "This is the very end of the 11th story of Rebbe Nachman of Breslev's *Sippurei Maasiyot*, "Of the King's Son and the Maid's Son Who Were Switched." This was a special method of story-telling that Rebbe Nachman used, sort of a spiritual 'trick' that he learned from his great-grandfather, the holy Baal Shem Tov. The stories, essentially hints and clues about the geulah, penetrate the reader's/listener's soul on a subliminal level. These stories open clogged spiritual channels impenetrable by 'conventional' lessons and talks.

"The basic plot is summed up in the title. But in the end, the real king's son faces the ultimate challenge that hitherto no one had succeeded in doing; and his success spells proof of his being the real king's son. And, there's the garden in the story that has various features of the Temple: the bed (that was in the Holy of Holies), the table, the menorah, and the chair. The real king's son succeeds in entering the garden and finishing the job needed.

"But notice the key phrase in the section on the note: 'slightly adjusted'. See, that's it. Everything is already there – it's all in the garden already. All the pieces are there, sort of like those of a big puzzle. But it is just slightly out of place – all it needs is a slight adjusting, a fine-tuning. The puzzle needs to be assembled properly so the picture can emerge.

"Honestly, I totally agree with your point before that everything appears to be total chaos. There isn't even one area in the world that isn't corrupt. And everyone knows it – Government, Medicine, Education, Media, Law, Religion, etc., etc., etc. But, on the other hand, the structures themselves are good and solid. And I don't just mean the building structures, though those are important too. I mean also communication systems and structures, and organizational and social structures. The people managing and running these structures and frameworks can easily be replaced. It's the structures themselves you need to look at. And when you really do, you'll see that they really only need a slight adjusting.

"What's more, do you know why all these institutions and systems are corrupt?"

"Really, why?"

"Because they all lack faith. That is the root of all corruption, the fuel of corruption, and the expression of corruption. Everything out there puts out the same corrupt message that is the polar opposite of, totally against and absolutely hostile towards faith, meaning that the heart of the matter is the underlying essential spiritual ingredient: faith. Real faith necessitates honesty, integrity, and 'Love thy Neighbor as Yourself'.

"Once we white-wash all these institutions and frameworks with real faith, the corruption will vanish by itself, just as rust, mold, rot, and mildew are gotten rid of with the proper physical wash."

Just then, the tip of another note surfaced at the rim of my bottle and they jumped, quick to see what it revealed.

> *And the earth was chaos and the spirit of God*
> *hovered on the face of the water.*
> *(1st Book, "At the Top" (Genesis) 1:2)*

"You'll notice," I said referring to the note, "that chaos is specifically pinned on the earth alone – it did not pertain to or have any bearing on the heavens.[3] And this dis-order seems indicative of all of existence – meaning, everything was there, just not in their proper places. This funnels down and becomes an on-going motif throughout the history of existence."

"Hey, question," Aryeh Lieb sat up to ask. "Why did He design existence this way in the first place?"

"Good question. But how about we get a little shut eye and take it up in the morning?" I answered, fixing my bed roll. But I did let them peek and check in again with the special bottle I brought with me.

> *1. Know, that before the emanations were emanated and the creatures were created, the upper simple Light had filled the entire existence, and there was no empty space whatsoever, for everything was filled with that simple, boundless Light. And there was no such part as head, and no such part as tail; that is, there was neither beginning nor end, for everything was simple or smoothly balanced evenly and equally in one likeness or affinity, and that is called the Endless Light.*
> *(Rabbi Isaac Luria, the holy "Ari": Etz HaChaim part 1).*

---

3   See "Besha'ar HaArmon", the Introduction to Rabbi Moshe Chaim Armoni's *Bati LeArmoni*, vol 1 of the series.

DAY

CHAPTER 3

The morning air at dawn is refreshingly cool and calm. Aryeh Lieb was already stoking a new fire with coffee cooking – straight black. No sugar or milk in this neck of the woods. And Dan Shimon was playing audience. "Good morning," we all got a round going to each other.

"How did you sleep?" I was asked.

"Hard and well, thank you," I answered with a smile. "Such peace and peace-of-mind out here. It's wonderful."

"Normally so," Aryeh Lieb chimed in.

"Oh?" I asked concerned.

"Well, after an evening like we had, do you think I'd be able to get my mind off to sleep?!" Aryeh Lieb explained in a tone of mock-accusation.

"I second the motion," Dan Shimon voted.

"I'm truly sorry if I only brought discomfort with me," I proffered.

"Heck no," came their response. "Don't be sorry. It was a rather positive 'discomfort' if you want to put it that way." A pleasant quiet enveloped us. That fulfilling sense of understanding, the sweetness of acquired truth and knowledge, prevailed. Only the crackling of the fire and then the boiling of the coffee could be heard for a good long while.

"I would think," Aryeh Lieb finally broke the silence, "that as a truly good and law-abiding citizen, I would naturally abide by the Ten Commandments. I don't steal or lie." The subject was obviously weighing heavily on his mind.

"Lying is not one of the ten," I cut him off.

"No?"

"No. It's not. Not in the original – in Hebrew. And it's the original that counts."

"To say that you at least abide by the Ten Commandments would require you to believe in God – Numero Uno is 'I am the Lord your God…'"

"I can deal with that," he answered me.

"It would also require you to observe the Sabbath," I dared to add.

"Oh well," he said with a smidgen of that undertone that says 'I give up,' "I'm not much into organized religion."

"Are we back to that issue? I thought I closed that case. What does the Sabbath have to do with an organization – any one – buildings and membership dues? Facts are facts. It's Numero 4 on the list of 10."

"Only certain people observe it."

"But that's smack in the core of the illusion we discussed." He looked at me squarely. "If I recall correctly," I continued, "you once accepted a quote by Snoopy the dog. Truth is truth. Period." He looked at me annoyed at my reference and recollection.

"Tell me," I tried to brush over the aggravation I caused. "If truth were dressed in an outfit you didn't like, would you dismiss it?

"And that sort of reminds me," I went on, not letting him answer just yet. "Do you remember when Robert Pirsig wrote in his book *Zen and the Art of Motorcycle Maintenance*:

'The truth knocks on the door and you say, "Go away, I'm looking for the truth," and so it goes away. Puzzling' (p.13).

He encapsulates my point so well.

"I'm mostly just playing devil's advocate now, as the phrase goes. But really, what if truth – the one and only, Absolute Truth – what if it just happened to be dressed up as an organized religion?" I finished.

"That's a toughy," Aryeh Leib answered in all honesty.

"But that's precisely the illusion. You would be falling head-first and hard for the illusion if you'd reject it." He was silent for a moment. The wind blew a bit. And I noticed that my bottle resting on the table-rock blew over on to its side. I didn't know if Aryeh Lieb even noticed it.

"I guess," he started and stopped momentarily again. "I suppose I would learn as much as I could to know to separate the wheat from the chaff. I would take only the truth and leave the décor."

I gave him a truly heartfelt smile. I decided to take a chance with a bluff that he wasn't of the Am, or nation. "Now, after all that," I said pleased, "I'm sure you'll be relieved to know that you are not supposed to observe the Ten Commandments." He did show a sign of relief. "You are, however, required to observe the Seven Laws of the Descendants of Noah," I continued. He was obviously rendered dumbfounded and wasn't sure where he belonged.

"Oh?" is all he could think to say.

"Yes," I began. "You're not allowed to worship idols."

"No sweat," he cut me off with light chuckle.

"Nor murder or steal."

"Of course not," he affirmed.

"Or eat a limb of an animal while it is still alive."

"Yuck! I wouldn't anyway," he assured.

"Or curse God or commit adultery," I continued. "You are, however, and that means within a society, of course, required to appoint judges and set up courts of justice."

"Society is pretty much doing that for me already," he commented. "That's it?"

"That's it," I replied.

"Can do."

"Good."

"Oh," I remarked, as I remembered. "Did you know that these Noahide Laws, as they call them, are actually recognized by US Law?"

"What do you say?"

"Well, both Houses of the US Congress passed a Bill in 1991, declaring these 7 Laws of Noah the basis for ethical conduct in our civilization."

"I didn't know."

"So much for claims of being a good citizen – at least an informed one," I said to him with a half-smile, which he returned.

GOD

CHAPTER 4

"You know what?" I began, but didn't give either of them time to respond. "I'm going to offer you an additional note of consolation to your 'thing' over all the corruption. Actually, to put it more correctly, your consolation prize is really THE first place grand prize."

"What's that?"

"The fact that you live here in the Land of Israel." I was groping for the means to connect with them from another bluff, the other way around, assuming they are from the Am.

"But we're in the US now," one said almost to himself.

"Your bodies," I replied. "Not your souls."

"True," he said yet softer. "We're actually in Israel."

"Oh, man, talk about third-world-style corruption! –" the other was already getting worked up.

"I know. I know. That is part of our trial. Look, for 2000 years we've yearned and prayed to be able to come home from exile to the land promised to us. Here WE are right now, right here, right in the very Land of Israel, but in spiritual exile, while most of Am Yisrael stays out in the diaspora. Who would have believed that when we finally get the ability and opportunity, that so many – too many – of our nation would opt to stay in La La Land?! We're like a bunch of sleep-walkers, zombies!

"And you know how it is anywhere else in the world, on

any other soil: The minute we start feeling too much at home, the gentiles remind us that we're just visitors. Oh, they remind us alright. Even after we've been in a place for generations, it's pogroms, decrees, the Holocaust – "

"But where's the consolation you promised?" A note's corner became visible. And a string of two notes came up.

> *Forever should one live in Eretz Yisrael even in a city whose majority is idol-worshippers and not live in the diaspora and even in a city whose majority is Yisrael*
>
> *Whoever lives outside Eretz Yisrael resembles one who has no God, while whoever lives in Eretz Yisrael resembles one who has a God*
> *(Tractate Ketubot 110b)*

> *In Eretz Yisrael one can perceive more clearly than anywhere else the direct providence of Hashem – hashgaha pratit...*
>
> *The influx of holiness into people's minds is different here, in Eretz Yisrael. If a person is willing to think deeply about Torah in Eretz Yisrael, he will find his efforts rewarded with a flow of ideas much deeper and more abundant than he would achieve with the same effort elsewhere.*
> *(from Rabbi Eliyahu E. Dessler's Michtav Me'Eliyahu[4])*

"And it's more than just that. As of the writing of this right now, if you check out the statistics, the latest of which are from 2014, you'll see that the Jewish population in Israel is approaching

4   in Rabbi Aryeh Carmell's *Strive for Truth* part 6, Parashat "Ekev" p.114.

43% of the total global Jewish population."

"Okay. So?"

"So, it's getting pretty close to the 50% mark and then past it. It's already 2016 and aliya is up and Israel has the highest figure on the stats list. Israel and the US together have close to 85% of the world Jewish population; but Israel is number one."

"And that means what?"

"That means that we are oh so close to finally having the majority of the Nation of Israel back on the soil of the Land of Israel."

"Okay. I can feel your hype. But spell it out for me. I'm not totally following." And with that, a longer string of notes poked up.

> *You do not have a truma [contribution] by Torah unless in Eretz Yisrael only and the time that all of Yisrael is there.*[5]

> *At this time...there is no obligation for trumot and maaserot by the Torah, rather by their words [our Sages']. Because it is said: That you should come, meaning all of you coming and not just a small number of you coming.*[6]

> *And this mitzvah [of building the Beit HaBehirah] is practiced at the time that most of Yisrael is on its land.*[7]

---

5   Rambam [Maimonides] *Seder Zraim, Halachot Trumot*, chapter 1, 26.
6   *Shulchan Aruch, Yoreh Deah, Halachot Trumot veMaaserot*, section 331, verse 2
7   *Sefer HaChinuch*, end of section 95.

> *As is the opinion of Maimonides z"l who wrote that the mitzvot of trumot and maaserot by the Torah is only at the time that Eretz Yisrael is settled by [Am Yisrael].[8]*

> *The Yovel [Jubilee] is practiced, as the Talmud teaches, for all its settlers at the time its settlers are appropriately so [most] and not at a time that they [Am Yisrael] are mixed [throughout the Diaspora].[9]*

> *RUBO KEKULO ['all' of Am Yisrael means 'most' of it and vice versa][10]*

"Actually, I'm saying a couple of things here. First of all, it means that so long as we are not 'most' of us here, we are not performing these mitzvoth by Torah, mideOrayta. And – "

"Wait. So you mean to say that all this time, Am Yisrael wasn't 'really' getting credit for them, so to speak and doing them for real? Like, illusions?"

"Credit yes. But done for real, well…I don't mean to disillusion you too hard, but let's just say that it's been more like a continuous dress rehearsal since our exile 2000 years ago. The mitzvoth done per our Sages, '*mideRabbanan*' as opposed to done per the Torah being '*mideOrayta*', are mitzvoth only in their practice form. Only once they go to the level of *mideOrayta* are they the 'real thing'. So now do you get it?

"**It's already a different ball game living here in the Land of Israel. But once MOST of Am Yisrael gets here, lives here, it bumps up to a totally different league. Today we are so close**

---

8   Ibid. Section 78.
9   Tractate Archin 32b.
10   Tractate Horiyot 3b, Tractate Hulin 70a, Tractate Nidda 29a.

to it already. But once we attain the statistical status of 'rubo' meaning the majority of the nation here, that will be the game changer completely. By definition of Torah, that will begin God's New World Order.

"That's why it's so hard to understand how most of the Am is stuck in La La Land. It's the weirdest thing. Everyone's just going about their own personal business, while everyone's waiting for someone to do something. La de da. Status quo. And of course, nothing really happens and no one really does anything. La de da.

"Well, WAKE UP, AM YISRAEL!!! Smell the coffee and check your GPS!"

Wake up, everybody! Time to pack up & come home!

CHAPTER 5

I t's amazing. Fascinating really."

"Something fascinating? Something real?"

"No, really. Seriously. You can truly see the collective consciousness gravitate toward our destination, toward The New World Order. People find themselves talking and thinking of an impending New World Order, because the soul, the collective soul, knows that we are all destined for the final redemption and the coming of the Messiah. They also talk of a Zombie Apocalypse, because the soul perceives the truth of the prophesized Resurrection of the Dead."

"What do you mean?"

"You know how when you first wake up, you're a little stiff?'

"Yeah."

"Well, our collective consciousness has been much the same. Over the last century, it's shown that it senses this new way of the world, on an internal, metaphysical level. There's something in our spiritual-metaphysical DNA that yearns for it.

"Take for example Communism. Millions got swept up in it because of its concept that everyone should receive exactly what they need. This is a basic concept of the Thought of Creation."

"What about Socialism?"

"The collective soul felt the pull as per God's saying –

A world of good-will will be created
(Psalms 89:3).

"And Fascism?"

"The soul feels that there's something bigger, that it's part of and a part of this greater entity. And the soul is up and willing to submit, even sacrifice itself, for this grander ideal."

"And the bonus question: What about Democracy?"

"Democracy is a different sort of bird. The others we mentioned aim towards God's New World Order, but they're false prophets. Democracy is a different creature, mostly because it doesn't take away the individual's free will. Yet it's more than that.

"At the root and essence of Democracy is the belief in the existence of certain 'natural laws' – whose source is in God. It being an eternal, God-given law, we may also see it swing into the realm and be called metaphysical law too. But what is important is that Democracy, by definition, is a means to a higher end and not an end in itself. It does not stand above moral values, nor are any of the freedoms it provides the individual absolute. That is why what remains continually debated in democratic countries is what it defines to be moral and who has the right to establish that. And this changes. Nonetheless, it is accepted that these certain moral values are above Democracy and that the latter per se is not the highest of values.

"So, democracy and God's Law, Torah, are not in competition or opposition. In fact, human beings' natural, inalienable right is free will; and free will is precisely the essential key of God's Thought of Creation. So, any regime or social structure that impedes free thought or impinges upon our faculty of choice is plain and simply bad and wrong. Democracy is a means to enable the individual to believe and worship as he or she pleases. Moreover, most of the moral values that the democracies of the world today uphold are already based on Torah: not to steal, not to murder, etc.

"What that means is that democracy is in sync with our pull toward God's New World Order. Democracy provides a means for upholding the morals of Torah. Moreover, Torah already affected democracy, the will of the majority of the people, in many areas, like city municipal management, establishing goals and priorities, and city economic and social development."[11]

"But getting back on track, all these man-made systems and concepts all prepared us and let us progress one step forward, because each introduced one aspect of the greater, true plan, and made us conscious of that one particular part. On the other hand, it's like we've still collectively lost our spiritual compass reading. Have you ever been to the Burnt House Museum in the Old City of Jerusalem?"

"Yes – No," came the chorus of replies.

"Well, to whichever voice of the chorus that was the source of the No, then, may I recommend that you go. It's located in the Old City of Jerusalem, very near the Temple Museum. Actually, I urge you to visit both places. But, back to the Burnt House Museum, it's an excavated house from the Second Temple period that had been set on fire during the Roman destruction of Jerusalem and had been inhabited by the Kathros Cohen family. What mostly comes to mind now, and why I'm mentioning it, is that in one part of the dramatized movie they show of the Kathros family, the wife is talking to the young Israelite girl working for her. The girl speaks with fear of the looming destruction and doom. The Cohen mistress of the house merely comments, "Nothing will happen to us. We're Cohens."

Why is it we never seem to read the road map before it's too late?! Today, to cater to our laziness, the GPS even talks to us, tells us out loud and clear: 'You are here; and you are headed in this direction.' When will we ever learn? When will we figure out where we are? Where we need to be? And why?

> They [Am Yisrael] denied God and said, 'He is not,
> and the evil will not come upon us, and the sword
> and famine will not be seen
>
> (Jeremiah 5: 12).

"What if they opt to stay in their sleep-walk mode, in La La Land?"

---

11 See Tractate Brachot 55a

"They won't."

"How can you be sure? The words of the prophets?"

"That too."

"Too? Whose else?"

"God's."

"Oh."

"The entire story of Eliezer's mission in chapter 24 of Genesis is actually all about this. You'll notice that Yitzhak, Isaac's name in Hebrew, is in the future tense: he will laugh. And, as many like Rashi have pointed out, this section of God's normally-terse, lean-and-mean word appears uncharacteristically wordy and repetitive. But what we learn is that the match-making and marriage of Yitzhak and Rivka are far from a personal tale – it is the description of the nation at large, the entire sequence of its history, including the receiving of the Torah at Revelation, and the final outcome, the coming of Mashiach.[12]

"On one level, Isaac represents the soul, and Rebecca the body. On a parallel level, the couple represents the relationship between God and the Nation of Israel. Eliezer asks Abraham, his master, 'Maybe the woman won't be willing to follow me' (verse 5), meaning 'Maybe Am Yisrael won't want to go towards the *geulah*, the final redemption; maybe the time hasn't come (to get married/for Mashiach) or that it's better for them to remain in the Diaspora.' So Eliezer continues and asks, 'Should I bring your son back to the land?' To this, Abraham answers,

> God, the God of the heavens Who took me out of my father's house and from the land [where] I was born and Who spoke to me and swore unto me saying 'To your seed I give this land', Who will send His angel before you, and you will take a woman for my son from there
>
> (At the Top (Genesis) 24:7).

"So the answer to the question was basically No."

---

12 Rav Moshe Chaim Armoni's *Bati LeArmoni*, parashat "Chayei Sarah" pp. 114-117.

"To the question on its basic, literal level, correct. But the answer is hardly only that. The 'angel' that Abraham tells Eliezer will go before him is Elijah the Prophet, who is promised to precede and herald the coming of Mashiach, the Messiah – that's the info he's getting across. Then, after that, Abraham seems to ask again only a little differently: 'And if the woman isn't willing to follow you, and you are cleared of this my oath' (verse 8). What this means is: And if, even after all the signs that Yisrael receives, Am Yisrael still isn't willing for the redemption, their desire for it to actually come is insufficient, and they are content in the Diaspora – "And you are cleared of this my oath" (i.e. harsh *dinim* will befall Am Yisrael, God forbid").

"Meaning all the nasty stuff that happens."

"Right, for the purpose of waking up Am Yisrael out of their stupor in staying away from God's Promised Land."

"In La La Land."

"Exactly. Just where the nation is now, physically and spiritually. But then, look when all this happens. Look what it says: 'At the time of the evening' (verse 11), being the eve of the end of the exile. 'At the time that the well-drawers come out' (ibid, continued). Torah is called water; and the well-drawers are the Torah scholars who study the holy Torah at the time of the end of our spiritual exile, the eve of the redemption. Meaning, NOW. This is where we are right now. Just as a GPS would indicate.

"Also, notice the words "And the daughters of the people of the city come out to draw [from the well]" (verse 13), in the original Hebrew, the words comprise the acronym of Elijah – the one who will herald in the redemption. And then "The man wondering at her" (verse 21); in Hebrew, Mishtaeh, comprises the letters of et Moshe, meaning [it being] Moses, whose second coming before the Redemption is to clarify the Erev Rav from the Nation of Israel.

"But then, the long and the short of it is, as everybody knows, that Rivka does follow Eliezer back. This is how God tells us that it's gonna happen, one way or the other. So, we know that Am

Yisrael will come back. After giving His word of this in the Torah, later on, God kept sending prophets to remind us, even as we were heading o ut yet again into exile. All these messages. So we wouldn't forget and we wouldn't misunderstand.

- And He will raise a miracle to the nations and will assemble the remote of Israel and the dispersed of Judah and will gather from the four corners of the earth (Isaiah 11:12).
- And will be said on that day 'Here, this is our God for Whom we have hoped and for Him to rescue us. This is God; we have hoped for Him; we will rejoice and be happy in His salvation (ibid 25:9).
- Do not fear because I am with you; from the east I will bring your seed, and from the west I will assemble you. I will tell the north 'Give' and to the south 'Don't imprison, bring My sons from afar and My daughters from the corner of the earth' (ibid 43: 5-6).
- 'You are my witnesses,' said God, 'and my servant whom I have chosen in order for you to know and believe in Me and to understand that I am He, before Me was not formed a god and after Me there will not be' (ibid 43: 10).
- Because, as God lives, Who has raised and Who has brought the seed of the House of Israel from the north land and from all of the lands where I have driven them there and they dwelt on their own soil (Jeremiah 23: 8).
- 'And I will be found by you,' said God, 'and I will capture your captivity and gather you from the nations and from all of the places where I have driven you there,' said God, 'and I have brought you back to the place from where I have exiled you' (ibid 29:14).
- Thus has God said, 'A voice in Ramah is heard, bitter crying, Rachel crying for her children, refusing to be comforted for her children, because they are not.' Thus has God said, 'Refrain your voice from crying, and your eyes from tear,

because there is reward for your action,' said God, 'and
they will return from the land of the enemy. There is hope
for your future,' said God, 'and sons will return to their
own borders' (ibid 31: 14-16).

- I hereby gather them from all of the lands where I have
driven them there in My ire and in My wrath and in great
rage, and I will return them to this place and I will have
them dwell in safety (ibid 32: 37).

- And the seed of Jacob and David My servant I will despise
from taking from his seed rulers over the seed of Abraham,
Isaac, and have mercy on them (ibid 33:26).

- 'You, don't fear, my servant Jacob,' said God, 'because with
you I am because I will make an end in all of the nations
that have driven you there and of you I will not make an
end, and I will suffer you to the law and clear I will not
clear you' (ibid 46:28).

- Therefore say, 'Thus said God, "I will gather you from the
nations and assemble you from the lands among which
you have been scattered and I gave you the soil of Israel
(Ezekiel 11:17).

- And I will take you out from the nations and I will gather
you from the lands in which you've been dispersed, with a
strong hand and an outstretched arm and with ire poured
out (ibid 20:34).

- And you will know that I am God in My bringing you to
the soil of Israel to the land to which I have lifted My hand
to give it to your fathers (ibid 20: 42).

- And was the word of God to me to say, 'Son of Adam, put
your face to Jerusalem and preach to the holy places and
prophesize to the soil of Israel' (ibid 21: 6-7).

- And I will take you from the nations and I will gather you
from all of the lands and I will bring you to your own land
(ibid 36: 24).

- And I made them into one nation on their land, in the

hills of Israel, and one king will be for all of them for king, and there will no longer be two nations and they will not be divided anymore into two kingdoms anymore…And I will purify them and they will be to Me a nation, and I will be for them [their] God. And my servant David king over you and one shepherd will be for everyone, and by My Law they will go and My statutes they will keep and do them. And they will dwell on the land that I gave to my servant to Jacob where dwelled on there your fathers and dwelt on it therein their children and the children of their children forever, and David my servant will be *nassi* [prince] to them forever. And I will make with them a covenant of peace, an everlasting covenant will be them, and I will give them and multiply them and give my Temple among them forever. And My dwelling will be on them and I will be for them [their] God and they will be unto me [My] people. And the nations will know that I God sanctify Israel in being My Temple among them forever (ibid 37: 22-28).

"Remember how after Jacob had been long enough in the diaspora, God reveals Himself and tells him to return home?"

> And said God to Jacob, 'Return to the land of your fathers and to your homeland and I will be with you'
>
> (At the Top (Genesis) 31:3)…
>
> Now get up, go from this land and return to your homeland
>
> (ibid 31: 13).

"So Jacob gives his wives the message telling them –"

> You know that I have worked with all my energy for your father. And your father has deceived me and changed by wages ten times over
>
> (ibid 31: 6-7).

"Isn't that just like the very story of our lives in exile?

Time to wake up, Am Yisrael! Time to come back home!

"Tell me about God's New World Order."

"Well, for one thing, under The New World Order, we will rid ourselves of all signs and trappings of our spiritual exile. Even the particular garb of the diaspora, needed at the time back when for the sake of survival in our physical exile, will fall way to our return to our native attire – that of the Land of Israel. This will include the Hassidic garb, which is actually that of Eastern Europe and particularly of the Polish aristocracy of the 17th century. And this will also include the men's necktie, which is the *gartel* of Edom that separates the head from the heart. The Jewish gartel is totally different, aimed to separate the upper body from the lower. And, yes, I do mean we'll return to the likes of Kamiz, Dishdishe, and Jalabiya and turbans."

Renew our days as of before

(Lamentations 5:21).

"We say that verse in our prayers all the time. It's time we promote our prayer up from the level of talk-the-talk to that of walk-the-talk."

"Well, tell me more. What will it be like?"

"Everyone will be on a higher consciousness and spiritual level. We'll all perceive God. Nature too, and all the laws of physics will be on a higher level. Would you like me to show you some pictures?"

"Are you kidding? I'd love to."

"Okay. Here you are. I have them in a special album, labeled 'Cameos of God's New World Order'" –

- The land will be full of the knowledge of God, as water covers the sea (Isaiah 11:9).

- Man to his neighbor will help and to his brother will say, 'Be strong!' (ibid 41:6).

- And the wolf shall dwell with the sheep, and the leopard shall lie down with the kid; and the calf and the young lion and the fatling will be together, and the little boy shall lead them. And the cow and the she-bear shall feed, together shall their young ones lie down: and the lion shall like the ox eat straw. And the suckling child shall play on the hole of the asp, and on the basilisk's den shall the weaned child stretch out his hand. They shall not do hurt nor destroy on all my holy mountain: for the earth shall be full of the knowledge of the Lord, as the waters cover the sea (ibid 11: 6-9).

- Then the blind will open their eyes and the ears of the deaf will be opened (ibid 35:5).

- And they will no longer teach man and his neighbor and man and his brother, saying, "Know God," because everyone will know Me, from the smallest of them and until the greatest of them,' said God, 'because I will forgive their sins and transgressions I will not remember anymore' (Jeremiah 31:33).

- And they [Am Yisrael] will be to Me [My] nation, and I will be for them [their] God. And I will give them one heart and one path to fear Me all the days to [make it] good for them and for their children after them. And I will make an everlasting covenant with them that I will not go back on after them, to do them good and that My awe I will put into their hearts so that they will not part from Me. And I will be glad in doing them good, and I will plant them in this land in truth with all my heart and with all soul…I will bring on them all the good that I speak of to them (ibid 32:38-42).

- And I gave them one heart and a new spirit I will put in their midst, and I will remove the heart of stone from their flesh and I gave them a heart of flesh. In order for in My statutes they will go and My laws they will keep and do them, and they will be to Me [My] nation and I will be to them [their] God (Ezekiel 11: 19-20 and 36:26-28).

- And I will raise over them one shepherd and shepherd you, namely My servant David...And I will be for them [their] God and My servant David *nassi* [prince] in their midst, I God have spoken. And I will make with them a covenant of peace and I will neutralize wild animals from the land, and they will dwell in the desert in safety...And the tree of the field will give its fruit and the land will give its crop, and they will be on their soil in safety and they will know that I am God by My breaking the rods of their yoke and make them succeed from the hand of those who had worked them. And they will no longer be despised by the nations and the animals of the land will not eat them and they dwelt in safety and with no dread. And I will raise for them a plantation of renown, and there will no longer be gatherers of hunger in the land and will no longer bear the disgrace of the nations (ibid 34: 23-29).

- 'Behold, days are coming,' said God, 'and I will send out hunger from the land, not hunger for bread and not thirst for water, but rather to hear the words of God' (Amos 8: 11).

- And will judge between the many nations and will scold great nations until far off, and they will pound their swords into plough-shares and their spears into pruning-knives, nation will not lift a sword to a nation and they will no longer learn war. And they will dwell each man under his vine and under his fig, and there is nothing of dread, because the mouth of God of Armies spoke (Micah 4:3-4).

- 'Greater will be the honor of this last House than the first,' said God of Armies. 'And in this place I will give peace,' said God of Armies (Haggai 2: 9).

CHAPTER 6

The next morning, I found my two new friends playing with their old illusions. Maybe it was just out of habit, but maybe they really did still hold on to the illusions as part of their beliefs.

"Whacha doin'?" I asked.

"Well, Dan Shimon's practicing floating a Phillips screwdriver for his own amusement. And me, well, I'm working on floating nine-sixteenths end-wrenches in the air plus evaporating clouds," Aryeh Lieb answered matter-of-factly. Dan Shimon sat a little farther off and was totally engrossed in his endeavors.

"I see. Only very specific end-wrenches," I said, the irony lost on him.

"It takes tremendous concentration and energy," Aryeh Lieb explained flatly.

"That too I can see. But, tell me. How exactly does that get you closer to God?" He jumped, startled, and relinquished his attempt to rekindle his concentration.

"To God?!" he asked, his tone giving away his disbelief that God could have anything to do with such activities.

"Yes, God," I stated. "Sorry to disillusion you if you thought anything about everything is not connected, rooted really, in God. The question always is whether or not we make the connection."

"Oh come on, bro', it's not such a big deal," he tried a distracting attempt to laugh it off. But I wouldn't let him.

"Well, it sort of is. It got an entire generation off on this misguided direction. Granted, GPS's weren't out and available in the stores back then in the 70s; but the basic spiritual compass got out of whack."

"Even so, that was back then."

"But if you think about it, each generation builds on the one that came before, whether following in tow or rebelling against. Either way, it causes a reaction and recalibration from where it was before that."

"You know, I would love to learn how to levitate."

"Really?!" I said incredulous, "What exactly for? How will that make you a better person?"

"You want to tell me you don't think that some of the great Tannaim, Amoraim, and Rebbes even of late didn't do these kinds of things?" he volleyed.

"First of all, you need to be respectful, my friend. And secondly, the question is what they would do such things for." He apologized softly under his breath. I continued, "And thirdly, I highly recommend you check out the work of Basava Premanand. That will burst your illusions on that issue."

"Who's that?"

"Basava Premanand – he's known as the Indian yogis buster. He revealed how they really levitate in the Far East." But Aryeh Lieb was only half listening.

"I wonder if your wonder-bottle could give me a tip now," he mumbled as he fished around for my bottle. Finding it, he pulled the note waiting for him. It said:

> *Richard said to Donald Shimoda:*
> *I happen to be so spiritually advanced that I consider*
> *these tricks of yours mere party games*
> (Richard Bach's *Illusions*, chapter 3, p.49).

"Everything in this world needs to be in the service of getting us closer to God. That's really all it's about. And, as a matter of fact, that is actually the very essence of Torah in a nutshell. All the tricks and displays of 'Look at what I can do!' are meaningless and pointless if they are not undertaken with the intent and purpose of getting closer to God and of revealing His glory in this world.

"Take Basava Premanand for a moment. How do you think he got into working so hard at debunking all those fakers? Firstly, he told how initially he himself wanted to learn how to do those things and have those powers himself, for himself. It really was for no purpose but to show off and impress people. The Tannaim, Kabbalists, and tzaddiks did everything they did in the service of doing the mitzvot. And that in turn would necessarily be for the sake of God and the betterment of mankind."

"See, I totally diss your illusions," I said.

"What? Disillusions?"

"Yes. Exactly."

CHAPTER 7

Dan Shimon had evidently crept up unnoticed by us in the middle of our little banter and had been listening, for the most part quietly, as Aryeh Lieb and I talked. Quiet but definitely attuned and considering me. I turned to him. "Tell me, Dan Shimon," I asked him, "do you talk to God, or the Creator, or however you want to call Him?"

"Talk to Him?" he retorted, emphasizing his first word.

"Yes, talk."

"How do you even know that He exists? How is it you're so sure?!" he asked a bit upset.

I answered as calm as I could and in all truth, "Because I just spoke to Him myself."

His eyes opened as he looked at me hard. "I also just spoke to you," I continued. Now he pulled his head back a little exposing a double-chin, obviously dumbfounded. Only after a moment of silence elapsed did I allow myself to proceed, "Have you ever been to a butcher?"

Now he looked totally confused, "Yeah, but…"

I knew what he wanted to ask, so I went on not listening to him air his bewilderment. "Did you ever try to talk to one of the chunks of meat there?"

"What?!?!" he shrieked, more annoyed at the sudden discernment that he must be making conversation with a madman.

"Of course you haven't," I answered for him, "just as nobody sane and sound like yourself would either," I assured him more of the sanity of his conversation and conversation partner. He relaxed his shoulders, displaying an obvious sign of relief.

"And yet you have no problem talking to me," I went back to the unnerving mode of explanation. "Dan Shimon, I'm also a chunk of flesh, can't you see? Think about that. You know instinctively that you can talk to me, but you would never even consider talking to flesh of another form – the kind one finds at a butcher, to say euphemistically. And you know why?"

"Because you're alive," he answered as if the lesson now became too easy.

"Yes, but how is it that I'm alive and that I can talk to you?" I challenged him now. But he didn't answer. "Because the Creator, Who renews His creation every single day, gives me new life every morning when I awake. And it is He Who speaks through me. And, it should be only a long life, but once He decides to leave my body, then that's exactly what I, and everybody else in His creation, is rendered – just a body. No more capable of conversation than any of those chunks you saw at the butcher."

Dan Shimon looked at me, deep in thought and just nodded. A bird landed on a branch not too far from us and chirped, nodded his tail up and down, then flew off. It was as if that little feathered friend was sent as a living visual aid to demonstrate my point. It was as if it were trying to say to us, 'The Creator breathes life into me right now. Here, can't you hear me chirp? And here, watch me move and fly.'

"I don't mean to disillusion you (actually, I did!), but illusions are a huge part of this world, as they are in the service of assisting us with our tikkun, our karmic account. A person, or rather a soul, only really learns from experience, right?"

"Okay."

"Well, experience can come vicariously, while not actually physically happening to us. You read a book. You really get into it. You feel for the hero or heroine and vicariously go through the learning process they do in the fictional story. But you yourself come away with new insight into your own life. You see things differently, maybe learn an important lesson from that hero. So you change and thus succeed in effecting any level of tikkun. Thus your illusionary, vicarious experience effects real change in your soul."

"So, I can use the illusion to basically get things done without actually having to get dirty? Figuratively speaking, of course. Right?"

"Right. But notice that even your qualifier of saying its 'figurative', meaning a pictorial representation of something – that too implies an illusion. It serves us in understanding. Creating the pictorial representation of what is not illusion (and what is not is pure metaphysical energy) is big business. It's what makes up the arts in all of its forms, from the written word to Hollywood."

"Wait. Back up a second. What is NOT illusion is pure metaphysical energy?"

"Correct."

"That means that everything that is added onto metaphysical energy IS illusion?"

"Right again. Let's go back to the body: Without the soul, it's just a chunk of meat. And even that decomposes and disappears. Or, take electricity, which though it's invisible, is considered physical – of the physical world – but is just energy, so it can help illustrate. You perceive the existence of this energy, electricity, by the form of the receiver, the appliance. So, in a heater, electricity 'translates' into heat, into an air-conditioner it 'translates' into cold, in a lamp it's light, in a washer, drier, vacuum cleaner, it expresses itself accordingly. But it's defined by the vessel it flows into. Without the energy, all those appliances are rendered useless lumps of metal."[13]

---

13 See Rabbi Moshe Chaim Armoni's *Bati LeArmoni*, "Devarim" Parashat VaEtchanan, p. 50

Dan Shimon had been leaning against his Travel Air. Now he sat down next to the two-or-so-foot flat-topped rock we used as a table, and laid his right forearm on it as he leaned his whole right side. My bottle happened to be set on our improvised "table." Dan Shimon immediately noticed and pointed to it. "May I?"

"Whenever you like," I answered. He read the note that popped up –

> ***God's candle is man's soul.***
> (King Solomon's *Proverbs* 20:27)

He let go of it quickly as if the note was running after him. Then he changed his mind and opted for yet another.

WILL

> *Know, that all of our forefathers, prophets and saints*
> *would not have attained their elevated spiritual level*
> *if it were not for the fact that they walked with God,*
> *meaning that they spoke to Him all the time and for*
> *their every need, big and small, spiritual or material.*
> (from Rebbe Nachman of Breslev's *Hishtapchut HaNefesh*
> [Outpouring of the Soul], in the "Introduction")[14]

"Back on track of our discussion about talking to Him. Amazing," he said half impressed, half spooked. "But what if I were to argue that it's just the great power of the human mind?" he tested me. "Take a look at the computer. It's man-made and can even be considered of supernatural nature."

"Then I would argue back: Who created the great human mind that created the computer?"

"I see," Dan Shimon answered. "I also did mean to ask you what you meant when you asked if I spoke to Him or It?"

"You know," I decided to begin my explanation from a different starting point and angle, "it says that the Messiah will cause the mute to speak. That will be his main accomplishment and triumph. How do you understand that?" I set it up, emphasizing my final "that."

"The key lies in the word itself, in its original language. 'Messiah,' the word itself, comes from the root 'to speak.' And the word 'Messiah' literally means, 'one who causes to speak,' that is, causes others to speak." Dan Shimon seemed to like that, so I went on.

"But when I say 'speak,' I don't mean just any blah-blah out there. In fact, one can talk all day and way into overtime in meetings, presentations and other forms of spoken human interaction. One can even yap for hours on his phone, into the wee

---

14 Also see *The Writings of Rebbe Nachman of Breslev* ("*Likutei Moharan*") Part 2, section 100.

hours of the night. But if a person doesn't talk to Him," I continued emphasizing the last word and pausing for the effect, "– then he's defined as one of the 'mute'.'

"The more you know and internalize the fact that He is here right now and always, with us, right next to us, in us, and among us, the more that you'll feel Him and the more you'll talk to Him," I explained. "And conversely, the more you talk to Him," I continued, "the more you'll strengthen your belief in Him. And you'll feel yourself getting answers and understanding. Your faith and your talking to Him go hand in hand. Light cannot be learned – it must be experienced."

"Like type your question in google and then a note floats down from Heaven?"

"Obviously not," I answered, ignoring the sarcasm. "But there are answers that come so clear and quick, they're like one of those figurative light bulbs that go off in one's head. Or like a single frame cartoon, which, in that single picture and terse caption, describes an entire story. Or like the dead give-away in Henry James' *The Portrait of a Lady*, after the long book's tale, all it took was that one cameo scene where she stands and he sits, and it's all so clear.

"Of course, that would be the purpose – the real, inner purpose – of these cartoons and books: to illustrate how it can be done: how quick messages can get across, even big and involved concepts."

"Well, I don't know how good I am at composing liturgy," Dan Shimon confessed. "My muse doesn't flow with all those Thou, Thy, and Thee's."

"Forget them," I retorted incisively. "You're not supposed to. Just speak the way you would to a friend. That's how He wants you to talk to Him."

"In English?" he asked, not quite sure how or what to ask.

"Is that your mother tongue? The language you're most comfortable with?"

"Well, yeah," he answered with a great mid-west American accent.

"Then English, or rather 'American,' for you it be," I said with a big smile, happy to almost finalize the issue. I then continued, "Just put aside all you know – wisdom, knowledge and all – and get yourself into a mode of simplicity and spiritual innocence, and then talk."

"Simplicity and innocence? Or...spiritual innocence?"

"To talk to Him, you need to be in a special state of innocence, much like a child to a parent. You just can't approach with preconceived notions or street-smartness..."

"I don't know if I think of myself as street-smart," Dan Shimon cut me off to bid his correction.

"I don't mean that in a totally negative way," I started to explain.

"I think I get it, though. Do you mean, sort of tabula rasa? One needs to approach with a clean slate, as it were."

"Right. But it's also to be able to feel His guiding 'hand' – His response. Again, with all kinds of preconceived notions and street-smartness or 'markings' on your 'tabula,' you'd only be able to perceive yourself and not Him."

"I got ya."

"It actually entails an entire way of looking at and dealing with life."

"None the less."

Be

CHAPTER 8

I caught Aryeh Lieb humming to himself "On Top of Spaghetti" as he was busy working on his Fleet. On the second round of the little ditty, he even began to happily voice the words. For a moment he attempted to step it up and really bellow it out happily, but I guess the distance to remaining anywhere near on key held him back. So now, not loud, but aloud nevertheless, he went on "…all covered with cheese…"

He was just about to serenade the meatball, which I did hope was at least a parve soy one, on the verge of rolling off the table after the infamous sneeze, when he caught sight of me out of the corner of his eye. He sort of froze for a moment. I smiled to ease the awkwardness, and he immediately resumed the maintenance work on his antique biplane. In a moment, he then called over to me in an offhand-like manner.

"Tell me," he began, "I have a question for you."

I walked over, just a few steps to his plane and sat down on a rock-made-chair. "Shoot," I said.

"Why are we here in the first place?"

"In a nutshell?" I answered with a question.

"Alright," he acquiesced.

"In a nutshell, our purpose in the world is to reveal the existence of the Creator to the world."

He went quiet and raised both eyebrows to signal he was

considering that for a moment. In keeping to his silence, he pointed to my bottle that I was holding under my arm, to ask nonverbally if he could take a peek. So, in keeping with his library-like silence, I merely pursed my lips in approval and handed him the bottle. He lightly tugged on the note's end and looked at the lot-laid message:

> *Know, that one must always focus on the inner intelligence of every matter, and bind himself to the wisdom and inner intelligence that is to be found in each thing. This, so that the intelligence which is in each thing may enlighten him, that he may draw closer to God through that thing. For the inner intelligence is a great light that shines for a person in all his ways.*
> (*The Writings of Rebbe Nachman of Breslev* [*Likutei Moharan*] part 1, section 1)

At that point, Dan Shimon walked up next to Aryeh Lieb, and they peered at the note together. The two looked up at me, brows knit, obviously perplexed. "May we break out of the nutshell?" Aryeh Lieb asked with a half-smile.

"We may," I played along, then looked down, paused, and then looked up again but with a more serious demeanor. "We would need to start from the beginning," I began. "Literally from Adam."

"Sounds good."

"For a crash course, it goes something like this: Once upon a time, Adam was created.

"What you had were then two basic forces: The Endless Light of God and the Endless Vessel, being creation. The Endless Light is complete goodness, positive energy whose nature is to give and nurture and supply infinite, endless abundance from the totality of abundance, and, more simply, was complete. It lacks nothing – that is, the Endless Light lacks nothing but lack. So, it created lack, which of itself had nothing and so needs and wants everything.

And this Endless Desire to Receive, as this lack is called, is the Endless Vessel that was created to contain the Endless Light. To enable this 'filling up of the vessel,' if you will, God purposely made the world incomplete – i.e. containing lack – for the purpose of our doing what it takes to complete it. And because we want to give and influence and thus be like God, God provided us with the world where we can feel that ultimate fill, that awesome feeling of attained fulfillment and satisfaction in expressing our individual selves toward a job well done – the job that contributes to completing and perfecting the world.

"Adam's body comprised creation in its entirety. All of the souls which today are divided among the entire population of our planet, were all parts of Adam's body; and that includes all things from the inanimate, vegetable, animal, and human levels. Put differently, the souls of all the people, animals, plants, and things in the entire world today were once a part of Adam's body – each person, a separate cell of the native of Eden."

"Wait a minute," Aryeh Lieb stopped me. "I'm not much of a theologian; but I somewhat recall being taught way back when that Adam gave names to all the animals."

"Good," I answered. "That's right. But the inner meaning of that is explained as Adam identifying each of those animal qualities of inside, or within himself.

"You see," I went on, "Adam's body then was not of the flesh and blood our bodies are today." I held up my hand to expose my fingernails. "These," I continued, "our nails, are the only remnants of what he was once made of. Nail. A see-through, pure conduit for the Creator's emanating 'Endless Light.' He didn't even have a digestive tract as we have today. He would look at, or into, an aspect of Creation, and be nourished by it through seeing or perceiving it. As they say 'feast your eyes' – he would do just that, literally."

"Oh, come on," Aryeh Lieb cut me off again. "Even without 'Bible 101 For Dummies' I know, as everyone does, that Adam ATE from the Tree of Knowledge."

"Correction," I retorted, "the Tree of Knowledge of Good and Evil. And tell me, Aryeh Lieb, do you really think it's really all about him literally taking a big juicy bite?...a bite of knowledge?"

"Well…" he stammered.

"Everything then was of pure spiritual nature. Nothing material yet existed." I paused. "When it says he took a bite," I went on, "it means he fell for the illusion that there's good and evil." I saw him open his mouth to cut me off again, so I pre-empted his remark. "Wait!" I didn't let him voice what was obvious he would say.

"Before he 'ate it' and fell for the illusion, evil was only a potential and latent element in the then perfect, unadulterated world. It was only after he quote-un-quote 'sinned' that evil became existent and active. As they say, 'You are what you eat.' He then made it a part of himself – something that wasn't till then.

"Now, two things happened to his body after he 'ate' from the Tree of Knowledge of Good and Evil. For one, his body became totally dismantled from being the one, whole, composite essence of the Endless Vessel. He completely broke apart into pieces, or what's called 'sparks.' Each spark comprised a separate, and consequently separated, soul. Each cell of his body was a distinct soul; and when his body came apart, each cell, or soul, became a separate being. Trees, animals, plants, birds, people and on and on.

"The second thing that resulted was that the sparks of Adam's body fell into what's called the 'husks,' being the parasitic, negative energy that manifested as a result of Adam's connecting to the element of evil.

"By the sparks falling into the husks, they went from being transparent and pure conduits for the Endless Light. Each became encased in an opaque covering, which are the physical bodies – of the inanimate, floral, animal, and human domains – that we have and see today.

"Just as bananas have peels and watermelons have rinds, we have flesh-and-blood bodies that cover or encase our souls. Of course, you understand that our souls are not like fruit under the peels. Our bodies are the outer 'husks,' but our souls remain purely spiritual. That's also the source of our inner conflicts – that between the spiritual pull of our souls versus the physical, material pull of our bodies.

"The soul, our soul, is part of God. It's pure and clean and requires no work of completion, no *tikkun*. What does need *tikkun* are the layers of attire over the soul, being our thoughts, speech, and actions. These encasements are what need to be elevated and made spiritual to be aligned with the soul, which is already and always connected to God – like a stream forever flowing from the river it runs back into.

"Our human bodies are real – material and real. But they give the illusion that one body is separate from another, as they are physically. It would be as if a cell of the arm called a cell of the leg – of the same body, mind you – 'stranger.' Each cell of a body is related. That's the illusion.

"Do you remember Alice Walker's *The Color Purple*?" I then asked.

"Sure."

"Well, remember when Shug expresses this very concept to Celie? She says:

> I believe God is everything…Everything that is or ever was or ever will be. And when you can feel that and be happy to feel that, you've found it…[O]ne day… it come to me: that feeling of being part of everything, not separate at all. I knew that if I cut a tree, my arm would bleed.

"Beautiful," I concluded with a nod. Aryeh Lieb nodded back in agreement. Dan Shimon, who had been silent all this time just listening, must have felt a need and reached for my bottle. He pulled the jutting note and read aloud:

> *Any man's death diminishes me, because I am*
> *involved in Mankind;*
> *And therefore never send to know*
> *for whom the bell tolls,*
> *It tolls for thee.*
>
> *John Donne*

"The Creator deliberately created His world, our world, unfinished, so we would complete it. All the structures and frameworks are testimony of human ability. But what they also come to prove is that whenever anything or anyone is divested of God, the Creator, and God-fearingness, it inevitably and certainly plummets to corruption. We've had to see it all happen to believe it: We had to go the hard path and see by way of experience and 1st-hand trial, that this is so. All so we come to the conclusion that from our utter disgust of all the corruption, we choose the path God intended – basically, we choose God.

"See, there's also the problem that our perception is a bit warped from mythical stories we've heard from other sources. Western culture, for example, has made all of us picture in our minds King David within some kind of Shakespearean backdrop, like something out of Hamlet or Macbeth. King David was nowhere near being European. But that's created a picture and reality in our mind anyway. We need to remember this with all things too, because if anything, it's diverted our focus and concentration from what's real and what we need to be doing.

Just then that note submerged and the corner of another emerged.

> *I will praise the name of God with song, and will*
> *magnify Him with thanksgiving.*
> *And this will please God better than a 'shor par*
> *makrin mafris' [an ox-bullock having horn and*
> *cloven hoof(s)]*
>
> *(Psalms 69: 31-32).*

"I don't get," one said.

"Me neither," said the other. "What's the connection to what we were talking about regarding the Garden of Eden."

"Well, it is connected," I answered. "I guess the bottle just figured there was something additional you'd be interested in."

"What can I tell you? – For the life of me, I don't see any connection. And these verses aren't new to me."

"Me too. And I'm beginning to think that maybe I never really understood any of this stuff,"

"Maybe that is another point the bottle is trying to show you."

"That what we thought we knew, we really didn't?"

"Part of it," I answered.

"Because we have a couple threads going right now: King David, the Garden of Eden, and Adam," one summed up with a twang of annoyance in his voice.

"Okay, so what do the verses mean?" the other cut in to get straight to the point. Both were a bit on edge, sort of thrown off equilibrium from what's familiar. "So how do they tie into our discussion?"

"Right. So first, context. King David beseeches God, asking Him to hear his prayers and to accept them before Him better than a '*shor par makrin mafris*', meaning an ox-bullock having a horn and cloven hoof(s). In essence, guys, this is the source of the legend of the unicorn."

"Whoa!"

"Yup, I'm interested. Go on," the second agreed.

"I think it wants you to detach yourself from all the kids stories about unicorns first, so you can really take in the truth about it," I began. "We need to straighten out in our mind what we just spoke about regarding King David not being anything close to Shakespearean. Just as King David wasn't Shakespearean-like, so too the unicorn wasn't Disney-like. From there, we go on to see that there were actually two animals that were unicorns, meaning having a single horn on their forehead: the *tachash* and the ox-bullock that King David referred to. Both, however, are no longer. King David also expressed: 'One spoke God, two of this I heard' (Psalms 62:12).

The Talmud[15] tells us about the *tachash* that existed when Am Yisrael wandered in the desert for forty years. For the sake of having all the raw materials needed to build the Tabernacle, God created this reddish animal to make the coverings from. After the Tabernacle was completed, God rendered this animal extinct. The Talmud discusses just how much it could not determine what kind of animal the tachash was, as it was, quite literally, sui generis.

"Whenever and wherever the Talmud[16] discusses the *tachash* it also mentions the ox-bullock, and vice versa, because of their similarity in having that single horn protrude from their forehead. And, our Sages point out how the unusual grammatical structure of the word for 'horn' emphasizes its being a single horn. Anyhow, our discussion relates to the ox-bullock, because it existed in the Garden of Eden. In fact, the single horn was an expression of the unity of the world before the sin,[17] plus the fact that there was only one of its kind. Adam offered up this singular ox-bullock-unicorn as a sacrifice; and from thereafter the world would only know of its offspring, the two-horned ox-bullock. The two-horned kind as we know it is indicative of the disunity of our world after the sin, and the ever-present battle between good and evil.

"So, also from the opposite direction, the unicorn had no place in a world as it thus became after Adam's sin. After the sin, the worlds were divided and existence became a war between two opposite forces of the Evil Inclination versus the Good Inclination. Therefore, the number of horns basically mirrors the level of chochma, wisdom of the world; it indicates the consequence or outcome of our level.

---

15 Jerusalem Talmud, Tractate Shabbat, chapter 2, Halacha 3 and Babylonian Talmud, Tractate Shabbat, 28b.

16 Also Tractates Avoda Zara 8a, and Cholin 60a.

17 See Rabbi Moshe Chaim Armoni's *Bati LeArmoni*, parashat "Veyera", pp. 88-89.

"Many times you can see the concept of what I spoke of regarding the cells from the same body – of Adam – manifested in a different way. The different roles and inclinations people have are not by chance. Some people are more inclined to 'hands-on' work, others are the 'on-the-road' (legs) type, others the 'brainy' folk and even those with what's called 'vision' (eyes)."

"Cool," he said. I nodded.

"This does, however, bring me to another of the major points I started to make. Because of all this, our function on earth today is what's called 'the clarification of sparks.' When we clarify a spark, we raise it out of the 'muddy' husks, clean it off, and return it the Endless Light.

"With this," I continued, "the function of our physical world is to provide us with the opportunity for weeding out the sparks from the husks and returning them to their spiritual root. With that, they will be repaired. The world is basically our workshop or laboratory for repairing souls.

"In fact, this world is very important in that only here can we get 'work' done. Where else can we practice the Golden Rule, fulfill the Ten Commandments or the Seven Laws of the Descendants of Noah?..."

Dan Shimon suddenly shot up, eyes wide, "Wait a minute. I have a theory about that."

"I know," I quickly answered. "But just hold on till we get there." At first Dan Shimon looked astonished, but then raised his brows acknowledging that he should not have been so surprised. "Angels don't need our earth," I went on. "WE need it and WE need to live in it – in and among society – with our feet on terra firma to be spiritual and do what we came here to do.

"True, we need to take care of our lab and keep it neat, clean and tidy. But, still we need to bear in mind that this is not home – it's the workplace. And what we're doing here is like pulling vegetables from the earth and dusting off the adhering soil – to reveal or 'clarify' the wheat from the chaff.

"Are you sure you still want to remain out of the nutshell?" I asked them.

"Hey, at this stage, is there really any going back?" was the way Aryeh Lieb answered.

"Here here," Dan Shimon seconded. He then reached over for my bottle.

> *"Let us raise a standard to which the wise and honest can repair."*
> *George Washington*

"Alright, our world here is a lab," Dan Shimon announced to get us back on course.

"Well," I complied, "there's work and 'repair' to do on different levels. There's the macro level, which deals with the whole world as a whole. And then there's everyone's own personal work to be done, on an individual basis.

"Of course," I went on, "everybody is a project manager – of his own personal project. Everybody has to work primarily on himself. We all have negative traits that need immediate attention: anger, jealousy, hate, pride, etc. That's because everybody has an innate desire to receive. The object, then, is to turn that general pull or desire to receive all the time and only for oneself, into a desire to receive, but to receive in order to pass along, contribute our unique part, and share and give to others. We need to strive to turn ourselves into channels. A channel passes along at one end what it receives at the other. And like a pipe, the less it's clogged within itself, so to say, the more it can channel.

"Though it's a bit more complicated, because you need to keep your vision in two directions. One is the piece of the puzzle that is you, the individual, doing what you need to be doing in the here and now. And then there's the big picture, where all the pieces fit in together.

> *"There's a Hole in Reality Through Which We Can Look If We Wish."[18]*

> *But our experience of moment-to-moment decision making in this world is also limited. To illustrate this, let us imagine a map of a country covered by a sheet of paper which has only one hole in it. If we move the paper so the hole reveals one city, this is all that we see. If we move it to another city, the first city disappears. But we know that in reality there are many cities on the map; they just happen to be covered. And when we remove the sheet of paper, we shall see them all at the same time.*

> *This is our situation. In the world of space and time, the world is revealed to us moment by moment... We can see that time exists in order to give us the opportunity to determine the quality of our own being. We have the opportunity to create ourselves as spiritual beings, close to Hashem...[19]*

"The disillusion is that God has a master plan for this world. He created His entire creation based on this plan, and that master plan is the Torah. What's more, nothing has been changed about His plan and nothing will. Instead, we're just experiencing the whole thing unfolding.

"See, it's all in the way we undertake our journey. The manner by which we use our God-given gifts, our tools for this world, that manner is what determines whether we do our tikkun or not and whether we succeed or not. If we use our tools positively, to influence

---

18 The title of Chapter 10 of John Steinbeck's *Sweet Thursday*.
19 Rabbi Aryeh Carmell's *Strive For Truth*, part 5 (translation of Rabbi Eliyahu Dessler's *Michtav MeEliyahu*), *parashat Beresheet* pages 34-35.

in such a way that the world goes forward towards fulfilling the Thought of Creation, we succeed. But, if we use our tools negatively and draw the world that much farther from its ultimate goal, we fail. So, you could be an absolutely brilliant genius and use your talents to the max. But if it's to channel destructive negativity, then you've messed up your tikkun and have failed in it.

"So, you see, Dan Shimon, it really does matter if we do good or not. And first of all, there is the distinction. It's best when we enjoy connecting to the good and doing things that are positive and constructive. It's a win-win situation where we enjoy, benefit and complete tikkun."

At that point, Aryeh Lieb reached for my bottle again, and opened the note that had remained and continued where he had read earlier. He started to read aloud.

> *2. And when in His simple will the desire to create the world and to manifest the emanations…"*
> *(The Ari's [Rabbi Isaac Luria] Etz HaChaim part 1)*[20]

He stopped, and I saw him impatiently finger another note, and then continued.

> *3. Behold He then restricted Himself in the middle point which is in Him precisely in the middle…*
> *(Ibid)*

> *"Unanswered" Question No. 2: Why is the universe so uniform on a large scale?*
> *(Stephen W. Hawking's A Brief History of Time)*[21]

---

20 *Etz HaChaim*, part 1, *Hechal* 1 "*AK*" gate 1, branch 2, section 4 *Derush "Igulim VeYosher"*

21 Stephen W. Hawking's *A Brief History of Time: From the Big Bang to Black Holes*, chapter 8, p. 127).

Aryeh Lieb stopped again and began getting frustrated. The notes were popping up and then back down fast and furiously. He started yanking the moment his felt each new note emerge as if time were running out in an urgent, immediate need to find an answer. He resumed, but kept stopping and starting again, reciting only fragments of the sections he got.

> *4. And there have remained an empty space and a vacuum surrounding the exact middle point...*

> *6...after the restriction it drew from the Endless Light one line, direct from His circular Light above downwards, and it gradually descended by evolution into that hollow or vacuum. The upper head of the line was extended from the Endless, Himself, and it contacted Him. Verily, the end of that line below did not contact the Endless Light. The line was drawn and extended below, and in that vacuum He emanated, created, formed and made all the collective worlds*
> *(Ibid, Rabbi Luria).*

> *What do we really know about the universe, and how do we know it? Where did the universe come from? Where is it going? Did the universe have a beginning, and if so, what happened before then?...Someday these answers may seem as obvious to us as the earth orbiting the sun...*
> *(Dr. Hawking's A Briefer History of Time)*[22]

He stopped and looked at me. "I guess," he said, "the truth

---

22 Dr. Hawking's *A Briefer History of Time* chapter 1, pages 4-5.

needs to be a bit diluted in order to swallow it." I smiled and nodded at that.

"Did you really think you could crack the ancient writings on the Big Bang from one quick glance?" But then, sort of as an afterthought, he held the bottle again and took a quick peek, though read aloud again.

> *Human kind cannot bear very much reality.*
> *T.S. Eliot*

"So okay," I declared, returning to our crash course. "Here's a key: What we call 'good' is anything that brings man and our world to, or at least closer, to our goal."

"Our purpose being to clarify sparks," Aryeh Lieb verified.

"Exactly," I answered. "And 'evil' is anything that causes man or our world to become further distant from our goal. Pilots are supposed to be good with equations. So…

Good = getting closer
Evil = getting farther
Good = Light (health, happiness, etc.)
Evil = Darkness (disease, depression, etc.)

"And that's why evil didn't exist before Adam ate from the Tree of Knowledge of Good and Evil – because then there was no distance between himself and the Light. He himself contained the Light," Aryeh Lieb tested himself.

"Excellent," I applauded. "And do you remember that list of 'dos' and 'don'ts' we discussed earlier?" Aryeh Lieb nodded and Dan Shimon continued to listen attentively. "Well then, doing a 'don't' would put sparks back in the mud, or at least would cause them to stay there in the mud."

"In the husks," Dan Shimon corrected me.

"Correct. And by doing a 'do' or by refraining from doing a 'don't' gets them out. It's all an issue of staying focused on our purpose here." A couple of eyebrows rose at this point, and we sort of broke for a moment to absorb things.

"If you think about it," I just carried on, "since everything in our world has a soul – plants, animals, everything – then clarifying sparks is the ultimate epitome of 'Love Thy Neighbor as Thyself.'"

"So, the Golden Rule is more of a metaphysical rule than a social or physical one," Aryeh Lieb surmised.

"Well," I answered, "it's both. Concepts like that are true on different levels. The physical and metaphysical are connected and one influences the other.

"Another example," I continued, "take the two trees you knew from what you thought was just a story. Connect with the concept of the Tree of Life, and you bind your life with stability and constant, total positivity. Connect to the Tree of Knowledge of Good and Evil, and you connect with the illusion of instability and uncertainty – to a world that's good one minute and then bad the next.

"To 'die' is to sever oneself from the Tree of Life and succumb to the illusion – distance from the Light, darkness, evil, and all those other yucky descriptions."

"So you could have it where people could then be medically alive, but actually dead," Aryeh Lieb said more as a question to test himself.

"Exactly," I answered. "The illusion and its posse are very seductive. The purpose of evil is to tempt us and allow us to have and use our free will or choice. Evil plays an important role in the grand cosmic plan. Without the existence of evil, we would have no other choice but to do good. And that would take away the value and 'credit,' as it were, for what's good."

"So evil is good?"

"No. That would be absurd. I just meant that evil has a function, a purpose, in the plan at large," I tried to explain. "Evil is still the villain who gets shot at the end by the good guy. You see, it's like a role offered for a play. But anybody in their right mind wouldn't take that role. They'd pick to play one that gets rewarded and not punished. The role one picks entails consequences. It's not exactly like after a show, where all the actors stand in a row and take a bow together. Those roles are not real. I'm talking about the roles we chose in the real world."

"Oh. And another thing. Just remember that there are more layers of depth to everything we say too."

*

"What I'd also like to know is why we have to define the goal as finding a theory that unifies gravity with the other forces? Gravity only pertains to the physical realm, which is only part of the equation. The soul is not bound or limited by gravity, as spiritual-metaphysical energy is not either. Phenomena like memories, thoughts, fantasies, and dreams travel faster than the speed of light and are not subject to gravity, but they are prevalent in our world and cannot be ignored or left out of any theory of existence that purports to be all-encompassing.

"Actually, to put things in proportion, we'd have to say that the majority of "reality" is spiritual, non-physical, and therefore the bigger part of reality is not subject to gravity – and that is the clincher.

"Something else to notice: The Torah says, "And there was evening and there was morning, one day" and then the same for "the second day" and so on. Well, where I'm from evening plus morning only equal two thirds of a "day" when you define day as 24 hours. That means, to be a day as I heard it, it should read 'evening to evening' to define a day. So right away we need to know that terms are not what we're used to, and maybe they're not even on our terms.

"What we know of 'days' is based on the rotation of the earth in relation to the sun. But, heck, the sun and moon were only created on day four. That is, the defining agents we have today to determine night and day and the 24-hour period we know of as 'day', those measuring sticks weren't even around for the first couple of 'days'.

*

In 1993, Rabbi Aryeh Moshe Eliyahu ben Shmuel Kaplan's ("Aryeh Kaplan") manuscript, which discusses, among other topics, the age of the universe, was published by the Association of Orthodox Jewish Scientists. In his posthumous book, Rabbi Kaplan reveals a particular writing of "Rabbi Isaac of Akko (1250-1350) [who] was a student and colleague of the Ramban [Nahmanides], and one of the foremost Kabbalists of his time." In explaining Rabbi Isaac's writings, Rabbi Kaplan begins by saying:

> The *Sefer ha-Temunah* [written around 1270 and which, per Kaplan, "establishes the age of the world, at least according to some classical interpretations, at forty-two thousand years" speaks about Sabbatical cycles (*shemitot*). This is based on the Talmudic teaching that "the world will exist for six thousand years, and in the seven-thousandth year, it will be destroyed" [per *Tractate Sanhedrin* 97a]. The *Sefer ha-Temunah* states that this seven-thousand-year cycle is merely one Sabbatical cycle. However, since there are seven Sabbatical cycles in a Jubilee, the world is destined to exist for forty-nine thousand years.

Rabbi Isaac of Akko writes:

> One of God's days is one thousand years, as it is written, "For a thousand days in Your sight are as a day" (Psalms 90:4). Since one of our years is 365¼ days, a year on high is 365,250 of our years. Two years on high is 730,000 of our years. From this, continue multiplying to 49,000 years [7 years of 7 sabbatical cycles; each year being 1,000 years], each year consisting of 365¼ days, and each supernal day being

one thousand of our years, as it is written, "God alone will prevail on that day" (Isaiah 2:11).

Rabbi Kaplan basically spells that out for us:

> Rabbi Isaac of Akko writes that since the Sabbatical cycles existed before Adam, their chronology must be measured, not in human years, but in divine years. Thus, the *Sefer ha-Temunah* is speaking of divine years when it states that the world is forty-two thousand years old. This has some startling consequences, for according to many Midrashic sources, a divine day is 1,000 earthly years long, and a divine year, consisting of 365¼ days, is equal to 365,250 earthly years.
>
> Thus, according to Rabbi Isaac of Akko, the universe would be 42,000 x 365,250 years old. This comes out to be 15,340,500,000 years, a highly significant figure. From calculations based on the expanding universe and other cosmological observations, modern science has concluded that the Big Bang occurred approximately 15 billion years ago. But here we see that same figure presented in a Torah source written over seven hundred years ago!

In Dr. Hawking's book *A Brief History of Time*, the age that he gives the universe is only vaguely "about ten or twenty thousand million years (1 or 2 with ten zeros after it)." When one considers the vagueness offered by modern science compared to a thirteenth-century rabbi, the magnitude of such a statement is phenomenal!

Showing the complexities of such studies, Rabbi Kaplan also unfurls:

> There is a question as to which cycle we are in today. Some authorities maintain that we are currently in the second Sabbatical cycle. Others maintain that we

are currently in the seventy cycle. According to the second opinion, the universe would have been forty-two thousand years old when Adam was created... According to Sefer ha-Temunah, then, there were other worlds before Adam was created. These were the worlds of previous Sabbatical cycles.

Then, Dr. Gerald Schroeder[23] says, "The problems of our origins...consider[ed] solved by experts...in fact have *not been solved* and are not about to be solved, at least not by the purely scientific methods used to date" (25)...

> "the duration and events of the billions of years that, according to cosmologists, have followed the Big Bang and those events of the first six days of Genesis are in fact one and the same. They are identical realities that have been described in vastly different terms" (26).

> "Six 24-hour days elapsed between 'the beginning,' that speck of time at the start of the Big Bang, and the appearance of mankind, and, *simultaneously*, it took some 15 billion, 365-day years to get from 'the beginning,' or the Big Bang as astrophysicists call it, to mankind" (chapter 2,p. 29).

> "only if we practice an exercise in logic that we refer to as 'stretching time.' This is the very heart of the matter" (33).

But then we need to explain the dilation of time...

Stephen Hawking explains[24] that "time runs differently for observers at different heights in a gravitational field...time moves more slowly closer to the earth's surface. The stronger the field,

---

23   Gerald L. Schroeder, Ph.D. *Genesis and the Big Bang: The Discovery of Harmony Between Modern Science and the Bible.*

24   *A Brief History of Time*

the greater this effect...[Thus] the theory of relativity gets rid of absolute time (chapter 6, p. 47).

Our biological clocks are equally affected by these changes in the flow of time (e.g. between living on the top of a mountain versus at sea level)...In the theory of relativity there is no unique absolute time; instead, each individual has his own personal measure of time that depends on where he is and how he is moving (chapter 6, p. 48).

In chapter 8, "The Big Bang, Black Holes and the Evolution of the Universe," Prof. Hawking stages an interesting scenario, or "thought experiment" as he calls it: An "intrepid" astronaut stands on a star as it collapses to the final state of a black hole and the astronaut sends a signal to his home spaceship every second (and parenthetically, he's "intrepid" because he would know that the difference in gravitational pull from just the distance between his head and feet on a collapsing star would be enough to tear him to shreds the moment the star does collapse).

The claim is that "gravity slows time" and the stronger the gravity, the greater the effect. The astronaut on the star is in a stronger gravitational field than his companions in orbit, so what to him is one second will be more than one second on their clocks. As the star collapses, its gravity becomes stronger and time begins to "stretch", meaning that "[e]verything that happens on the surface of the star...would be spread out over an infinite period of time, as seen from the spaceship (p.80). The interval between signals from the astronaut and their arrival at the spaceship "would get successively longer". This even though we've been given the map-key here in advance: We know that one signal was transmitted every second, even if each was perceived only, say, every thousand (or million or billion) years.

This intrepid astronaut scenario puts a very important consideration at front and center stage: Point of reference it's called. In Literature, the reader is charged and challenged to assess whether or not the speaker or narrator is reliable or not, and even by what authority he or she speaks his/her point of view.

> Here's the point: The uber-ultimate of all omniscient and omnipresent narrators is actually the One telling the story for us – God!

> Psalms 90:4 "For a thousand years in Your eyes is as a day."

So, Schroeder goes on to explain that "Einstein demonstrated that when a single event is viewed from two frames of reference, a thousand or even a billion years in one can indeed pass for days in the other. That is, this difference in perceived time is 'relativistic time dilation', meaning the difference in perceived time, as opposed to the dilation that makes the first six days of Genesis reassuringly compatible with the 15 billion years of cosmology (chapter 2, p. 44).

Note: "A clock on the Moon runs more rapidly than the same clock when on the Earth because the Moon has less gravity than the Earth…[and] gravity is a key factor in the reconciliation between Genesis and the Big Bang (45).

So, "whoever was in charge recorded the passage of 24 hours per day. But who was there to measure the passage of time? Until Adam appeared on day six, God alone was watching the clock. And that is the key" (p.49).

"For the first one or two days of the six days of Genesis, the Earth didn't even exist! – the Earth was void and unformed (p.49).

"There was no Earth in the early universe…no common calendar between God and the Earth" (50).

"According to Einstein's law of relativity, we now know it is *impossible* in an expanding universe to describe the elapsed time experienced during a sequence of events occurring in one part of the universe in a way that will be equal to the elapsed time for those same events when viewed from another part of the universe… the absolute passage of time [is] a very local affair. Time differs from place to place "(50). "Einstein's law of relativity tells us that dimensions in space and the passage of time are not absolute. Their measurement is an intimate function of the relationship between the observer and the observed" (34).

So –

- "A billion cosmic clocks were (and still are) ticking, each at its own, locally correct rate. Universally, they all started at the Big Bang and, at the very same instant, reached the moment when Adam appeared" (51).
- "for the time preceding Adam, the Creator's own reference frame...viewed all the universe as a single entity" (52).
- "the reference frame by which those [six 24-hour] days were measured was one which contained the total universe" (p.53).
- "at the moment of Adam's appearance...the chronology of the Bible and the flow of time on Earth became one – the common space-time relation between God and man was [then] fixed" (52).

In sum: On the one hand, the physical matter that was created was at its densest level and thus had the greatest gravitational pull and thus "interpreted" creation as being 15 billion years. On the other hand is the account by Whose point of view is told in the first verses of Genesis – being God's. And God is not subject to gravity. And thus, from His stance, creation is instead six days – with the seventh day creating the spiritual concept of rest.

*

"See what I mean?"

"Yeah I do. A whole lot involved. Maybe too much."

"There is endless depth. It's just a question of how deep you want or probe to go."

"Alright. But, one smaller question: It says that the seventh day created the spiritual concept of rest. What does that mean?"

"It basically means that it's generally misunderstood that

because, as we say 'God rested', that we all rest. Instead, God created Shabbat as part of creation and by creating Shabbat He created the spiritual concept of rest, not just the physical one, which is also sleep."

'Rashi writes: "What did the world lack? – Rest...the sense is not that God completed His work *on* the seventh day, but *with* the seventh day...But don't think that Shabbat is a mere adjunct or finishing touch to the world. On the contrary, Shabbat is the final goal and crowning glory of creation. It is the true content of creation."[25]

25 Rabbi Aryeh Carmell's *Strive For Truth* (translation of Rabbi Dessler's *Michtav MeEliyahu*) part 4, 1st section on Shabbat, pages 3-4.

ONE

CHAPTER 9

L isten, a gut feeling tells me that there's more to this global division of labor than what we talked about before. There's got to be more to it than that, and you're holding something back about it. I would think that if there's a division on the physical-material work that needs to be done, then there's got to be the same kind of division on the spiritual-metaphysical level too."

"Bravo!" I marveled. "And on many points too. First of all, bravo on listening to your gut feeling – just listening to your inner feeling is good. Though it's not really your gut, but your soul. Regardless, it's wonderful that you're listening to it. And that's the next level of your bravo.

"Secondly, to everything on the physical level, there's a spiritual-metaphysical counterpart, just as in physics it's known that every particle has an antiparticle[26]. So, yes, just as the body is made up of different organs and systems, and the division of work is done according to the internal nature of each, so too on the metaphysical. Also parallel is how the parts, organs, and systems of the body all have their independent jobs, and yet they are reciprocally influenced by the functioning of all the other parts and systems. So too on the spiritual.

"But on the other hand, to a certain extent, the division of work on the spiritual level isn't of different jobs, but rather of different

---

26 Hawking's *A Brief History of Time* chapter 5, p.73

paths that lead back to an integrated, unified whole root source –
supposed to, at least, lead to the same place, spiritually.

"It's pretty much like in math. For some folk, the only way they
can solve the equation is by using long division. And some write
out the number to divide by on the right side and some on the left.
Some also prefer the shorter, more direct method. But as long as
you have a way to solve for X and get the same right answer, you're
okay. In Hassidism too, there are methods, courts, and sects,
because the holy Baal Shem Tov had sixty spiritual 'warriors' who
he sent out in different directions to spread the word, to rekindle
the old way, among dispersed Jewry. So we have a single source
spreading out, delegating work, only for the purpose of reuniting
back at the same place.

"Similarly, you absolutely, positively must read *To Cross the
Line With a Bridge*. It tells how Abraham basically split his kids up
in different directions to spread the wisdom he attained: Ishmael
later brought about the Koran and Islam, Isaac and Jacob, Torah
and Judaism, and the children of Keturah, the Veda and Hinduism
– the Brahmans from Abraham. They were not intended to
compete or fight with one another, but to complement each other
and work together at the common goal of serving THE One God.

"There's a kind of criss-crossing of recognition between
the Torah and the Koran, with the basic acknowledgement and
agreement by BOTH sides that the Torah was given by God and
is His Word. From the side of Torah, Rashi has a whole discussion
on Hagar's seeing the angel.

> And [Hagar] called the name of God That spoke to
> her, 'You are an all-seeing God,' because she said,
> 'Have I also seen behind me His appearance?'
>
> (At the Top [Genesis] 16:13)

Rashi explains that Hagar, Ishmael's mother, was used to seeing
angels in Abraham's house, in Abraham's merit, but that this time

she saw the angel that came for her. The daughter of Pharaoh, from the palace of the heartland of sorcery and magic, and here she was calling the 'name of God' – the very Tetragrammaton – in monotheistic belief in the one 'God of Israel'.

"And there is also mention of Abraham's introduction of the mitzvoth, the commandments, to Ishmael when the three angels come to his tent and he runs to welcome and show them hospitality. In a generation where there was no such thing as hospitality and they were right next door to Sodom and Gomorrah, here was Ishmael learning the revolutionary concept of commandments to the One God and welcoming guests and showing hospitality from the perception that all is God's.

> And to the cattle Abraham ran and took the tender and good calf and gave [the calf] to the young man, and he hurried to do so
>
> (At the Top [Genesis] 18: 7).

Rashi notes that "the young man" was Ishmael, and he was being educated in the commandments.

"From the side of the Koran, Mohammed's original vision occurred during the initial al-Mecca period, when peaceful coexistence prevailed between the Nation of Israel and the neighboring Arabs. The following suras express Mohammed's original vision:[27]

> Because the Torah came down only for the Nation of Israel, and for the Arabs the people of Mecca there was no book…Therefore I come to give you The Book in Arabic which is directed at The Book of Moses
>
> (Koran 46, 11-12; 6, 155-158; 68, 37).[28]

---

27 My freestyle translation to English from Efraim ben Yosef's *BeOhalei Kadar* [In the Tents of Kadar], where he translates to Hebrew from the original Arabic.

28 Ibid. chapter 2, p. 133.

I have a witness from [the Nation of] Israel who
testifies that the words of the Arabic Book are the
same as the words that are in the Torah

(Ibid. 46, 8:9 – 9: 10). [29]

Any doubt that you may have regarding religion,
ask the Children of Israel, because they know it, the
Torah, well

(Ibid. 10, 94).[30]

For the reason that their [the Nation of Israel's]
prophets and rabbis were given the Torah to keep, and
they testify to its veracity

(Ibid. 5, 44/48).[31]

Ben Yosef also proffers those aspects that demonstrate even
implied, complementary acknowledgement, by way of the Muslim
traditional practices during the pilgrimage to Mecca, al-Zafa and
al-Marwa.

Al-Zafa and Al-Marwa are ceremonies of God,
therefore any pilgrim to the House [Kabah] for the
holiday, it will not be a sin upon him if he circles both
of them

(Koran in Sura 2, The Cow, 158).[32]

Ben Yosef points out that Mohammed's reference to "sin"
would derive from the Torah. These two locations were notorious
for idol-worship practices. The Torah forbids us to worship God
in places where idols abound and idol-worshipping is practiced.
Moreover, this tradition commemorates Hagar's flight from the

29 Ibid.
30 Ibid. chapter 16, p.607.
31 Ibid.
32 Ibid. chapter 11, p.450.

house of Abraham and Sarah and desperate search for water between these two hills. The Koran, in describing how it was Hagar that was sent from the house, implies the understanding that she was so by the mistress of house, Abraham's wife Sarah.[33]

"It was only at the later al-Medina period that the accursed Erev Rav and Crusaders incited Mohammed against the Nation of Israel. And if it weren't for their evil doings, I'm sure we'd still be enjoying peaceful, neighborly coexistence as we did during the original al-Mecca period."

"How could they do that when the verses and suras are written in black and white? I mean, the words are right there."

"My friend, that's pretty much the trick that many a good joke that floats around uses to reverse the meaning to get a good punch line. Only in our case, of course, it is so not funny. But it's much like an optical illusion, though in textual writing. Take for example the oxymoronic titles of Professor Raymond Smullyan: *This Book Needs No Title* and *What is the Name of This Book?*"[34] He smiled at this and then looked over to my bottle. Sure enough, a note was waiting to be pulled.

> *A grammar professor wrote the following sentence on the chalkboard and asked the students to punctuate it correctly:*
> *'A woman without her man is nothing'*
>
> *All of the males in the class wrote:*
> *'A woman, without her man, is nothing.'*
>
> *All of the females in the class wrote:*
> *'A woman: without her, man is nothing.'*

---

33 Ibid, pp. 450-451.
34 The full name is *What is the Name of This Book?: The Riddle of Dracula and Other Logical Puzzles*

AND

CHAPTER 10

Something on your mind. Something nagging you to say," Dan Shimon said as a half question-half statement.

"Actually yes," I answered.

"Not too good at hiding what's on your mind."

"I don't want to hide. Don't even try."

"So?"

"Well, earlier I used two terms that I don't like to use. Certain words and phrases I use figuratively just to get the point across, but I don't like them."

"Like?'

"Like 'devil's advocate' or 'tabula rasa.'"

"Tabula rasa? What's wrong with that?"

"It's an illusion."

"What? That's a riot."

"I don't know about a riot. Riots are disorder, and here I'm making order. Anyway, the only rasa part would be true in that babies born into the world haven't done any wrong…yet. They're clean, pure. But that's not how the term is used. As far as a clean slate is concerned, opened to influences and all – that's basically all an illusion." Dan Shimon shot a hard look with brows up and eyes wide.

"Each incarnation is a continuation of its preceding one. Each soul reincarnates into the very state it left off in in the last round. This is why people are born into different socio-economic conditions, with various fears, foibles, talents, aspirations and so on.

"What drives each and every one of us is our soul; and the soul is driven by its retribution – its very nemesis or 'Tikkun', literally meaning 'correction'. Each is here on his own personal agenda and for his own reasons. But that's why we're here in the first place – to take care of spiritual 'business'. It's what we need to work on or 'fix'. And it's this personal, spiritual business that makes us tick, causes us to do and go as we do, and is what drives us, consciously or not, and defines us. The soul may even drag the body along blindly so that it doesn't understand what it's doing or where it's going."

"So like Aryeh Lieb's love and drive to fly – "

"Engraved by some Tikkun he has and directed by a past life. What motivates people to do anything is their Tikkun."

"I'm sure Freud, Frankl, and Nietzsche would love to challenge you on that."

"Well let them keep feuding among themselves on the age old case of 'what makes us tick?', because, as you can see, they're basically wrong.

"Ditto for Joe Solomon, Ally Carter's espionage teacher at her Gallagher Academy:

> "There are six reasons anyone does anything: Love.
> Faith. Greed. Boredom. Fear…Revenge."

He forgot the main ingredient and the root that impels even the six he enumerated.

"Each on his bottom line theory that it's one main thing that drives us. There they're dead wrong. Each person is pulled by the dictates of the Tikkun of his own soul. So, okay, it could be based on various desires, like for power. But there are really almost an infinite number of possibilities.

"I can't promise, but I'll try to stay away from words I don't like and feuds," I concluded with a smile, which was promptly returned by Dan Shimon with a nod.

HIS

CHAPTER 11

Now, the Golden Rule had been a loaded issue between Aryeh Lieb and Dan Shimon.[35] The Golden Rule is golden because we are all related, part of Adam's original body. By being considerate of the other, we bring all of creation towards its goal.

But in Aryeh Lieb's (Richard's) book, Dan Shimon got Aryeh Lieb to surrender to the notion that the Golden Rule doesn't exist. Instead, he insisted, we are all free to do whatever we want to do, regardless of whether or not it hurts another. Of course, I absolutely and totally disagree.

"Imagine for a moment," Dan Shimon started to get riled up, taking a cue to revive the thought-form demonstration and point he made back then, "that some guy tells you that if he doesn't get a little of your blood he'll be hurt, physically and emotionally?" he summed up his old prop.

Aryeh Lieb raised his arms up while pointing his fingers down, "I've cuum to suck your blooood," he said with a smile, but doing a good impersonation nonetheless.

"No, Aryeh Lieb," retorted Dan Shimon rather annoyed. "He wasn't like that at all. He was actually quite...well, polite."

"Oh, hey, I apologize," Aryeh Lieb said with a trace of sarcasm as it occurred to him. "You're right. He really did ask nicely...that is...for my blood."

"He wasn't even out to kill you," Dan Shimon stayed his

---

35 Richard Bach's *Illusions* chapter 13

ground, still somewhat annoyed. "He told you that he just wanted a little bit."

"Yeah, yeah. Do you mean dot old wompire from Tronsylwania?" I played along, doing the best at doing a Transylvanian accent.

"Hey, that was pretty good," Dan Shimon graded my performance.

"Thanks," I tried to reply humbly.

"And you remember well."

"Could I forget such a scary sight? Guy with fangs, wearing a black cape with red satin lining, licking his lips as he approached Aryeh Lieb in the middle of the night."

"I don't know if it was quite the middle of the night," Dan Shimon said under his breath. "But it was definitely dark."

"Whatever," I acquiesced.

"Hey, you remember 'dot wompire,'" Aryeh Lieb chuckled.

"Do you think," Dan Shimon resumed, "that in a case like that the Golden Rule could apply? Nobody in his right mind would willingly let a vampire suck his blood."

"Well, maybe Bella Swan from *Twilight* would," Aryeh Lieb cut in.

"No," Dan Shimon said resolute. "She was a love-struck teenager and let him for different reasons. That doesn't count."

"Oh," is all Aryeh Lieb could say.

"Dan Shimon," I said, and maybe with too much force, "people willingly give blood all the time. And thank goodness – because that really is GOODness. That's what's called Central Column Energy – channeling or influencing goodness. Like you said, we're not talking about a case that would kill. But, would it be any different to you if the nurse, who takes the blood donations, were to wear a black cape with blood-red satin lining and stand at the doorway with her arm bent at the elbow, hand up, holding a huge syringe pointed up and ask, as a good-body donor came, "Ah, you've come to give me your blooood? If she did it that way, would it really make a difference? Maybe just externally, right?

"And what if you went like a good Samaritan to give blood

and found they decorated the ambulance marked 'Bloodmobile' something like the Batmobile?"

"You know," Aryeh Lieb remarked, "those two terms always did sound similar to me as a child. Funny you should mention it."

"In fact," I went back to the point I had been making, "don't people even donate organs?"

"So I'm supposed to give everybody anything they ask for if I have it?" Don argued.

"Absolutely not," I replied. "There's wisdom and common sense behind the grand Golden Rule." Despite his initial seriousness, he smiled in a way that meant something amusing just occurred to him, set off by something I said. "What?"

"You know what they say today in checking that term – that common sense isn't so common anymore. But it's always good to take it into consideration."

"Would that be like saying that the moral majority today is in the minority?"

"You got it," he replied and we smiled at that.

"Anyway, tell me, if an alcoholic asked you for booze, or a junky wanted money for drugs, don't you think you would be doing them and the world an awful disservice if you did? If you look at it truthfully, in instances like this, by giving you would actually be taking – causing those people to lose more of their life force and lose more distance from the Creator and our common goal. You see, here giving would be taking."

"So you perceive 'dot wompire' more like a positive recipient of a blood donation than a negative junky beggar?" Don asked.

"Actually," I responded slowly, "I was dealing more in general ideas, like that the need for blood is not necessarily negative. Each case needs to be considered separately. 'Dot' could be either. I would think that maybe to the good Dr. Cullen it would be one way, and to the savage James or Victoria it would be the other." He seemed to like that. "But, hey," I continued, "good point."

"Yeah," he agreed and we smiled.

CHAPTER 12

"Tell me something," Aryeh Lieb began. "You mentioned before this 'Central Column energy'. What did you mean?"

"Well, you already know that nature provides two basic energies, binary poles, positive and negative, Yin and Yang, male and female. And the whole world is an expression of the Desire to Receive at large, which is Left Column energy."

"What about energies? Like gravity? How does gravity fit into that equation?"

"Think about it. All movement denotes LACK, a Desire to Receive. Everything 'runs' to fill a lack, an emptiness, a vacuum, a void – to receive. So all energy in and of our world is merely an aspect of this same one metaphysical entity, an expression of the Endless Vessel. All four categories of force-carrying particles – the gravitational force, the electromagnetic force, the weak nuclear force (responsible for radioactivity), and the strong nuclear force[36] – are all expressions of this same Left Column-Desire to Receive energy. All four are branch-physical expressions of the metaphysical-root energy of the Endless Vessel, the aggregate Desire to Receive. So earth, the physical home of the Endless Vessel, the aggregate of all souls, would need to be compatible energetically – having a pull towards itself, toward its core. And that's what gravity is – an expression of this same Desire to Receive,

---

36   Dr. Stephen Hawking's *A Brief History of Time*, chapter 5, pp. 74-77

by pulling inward towards itself.

"But the Central Column is a special energy that we humans have the ability to create by virtue of our free will. This energy is not found in nature, in the physical – it's supernatural, and it becomes revealed when we use our Desire to Receive for the sake of sharing or giving."

"Then, where does it come from? How did we get this third energy, the Central Column?"

"Okay. Open up to chapter 22 of the First Book 'At the Top' (Genesis)."

"The Torah?"

"Of course. That's where it's all found and where it all began. But you know what? – Let's start with a little warm up."

"Exercise?"

"Spiritual exercise of our consciousness." He smiled. "Let's start with water and trees. Can you see how they fit into the category of what's living, growing, life-giving, nurturing?"

"Absolutely."

"In other words, they would be what?"

"I think I follow. They'd be Right Column energy – giving."

"The Desire to Give or Influence, the attribute of Mercy. Good. Now, what about fire?"

"Burning, consuming – Left. I mean, the Desire to Receive."

"Good. Also note that when fire consumes, it's red too. The attribute of Might (Gevurah). What about a knife?"

"Knives cut. So they usually end life or the flow of energy. I'd say, then, Left Column Energy."

"Correct. Also, because knives are Left Column, that's why Halacha states that we shouldn't hold a knife in our right hand when we bless. For example, if we bless on a fruit and hold it in our right hand, we should not also hold the fruit knife in our right hand as we bless, it's opposing energies. A few more spiritual calisthenics?"

"Sure. I'm game. Go ahead."

"Okay. Milk?"

"Well, it's life-giving or life-supporting. I'll say Right Column energy, of the Desire to Give."

"Good. Also notice that milk is white, plus the fact that the mother does not have to give up her life to provide milk. So, it corresponds with life and continuity."

"Gottcha."

"Meat? And, to make signs clearer, particularly beef."

"Oh, red. Then, Left Column, Desire to Receive."

"And note the concept of end and finality too. An animal ends its life to provide meat."

"True."

"By the way, these simple exercises also provide you with the basics and understanding of Kashrus and the Family Purity laws. Actually, most Halacha can be understood from this basic metaphysical law, like also Sha'atnez. Wool GIVES off warmth, and so we wear it in the winter, and it's ---"

"Right Column energy."

"Right. Well, no pun intended – correct. And linen, from flax seed, we wear in the summer because it TAKES away heat, and is thus –"

"I get you – Left Column energy."

"Nice. Also, note that shrouds are made of pure linen, whereas the *tallis* is made of pure wool."

"Ooh."

"Remember, in this world, these two polar energies are irreconcilable: Life and death, Right Column energy versus Left Column energy. They can complement in various ways and under certain, very particular and precise circumstances; but to avoid short circuits, they must remain separate. And metaphysical imbalances and short circuits do horrible things to mankind on an individual level, as on a collective one. Since the beginning of time, places and peoples that caused too much imbalance and too many short circuits brought on themselves catastrophic consequences: from the generation of Enosh, Noah, Sodom and Gomorrah, the Tower of Babel, ancient Egypt, Greece.

"You can think of it pretty much like in a battery. Each pole must remain at separate ends, although side-by-side they enable circuitry. Though sometimes circuitry isn't possible and just requires complete separation so there's no short-circuit. Like regarding Kashrus and Family Purity laws. Also Cohens, who correspond with the attrtibute of Mercy, Hesed, of the Right Column, are not allowed to enter cemeteries or have any contact with dead bodies, which are absolute Left Column energy.

"Colors and sources are just a few of the signs we are given to perceive the energies. But really, this is indicative of the larger scale too. The funny thing is that all the clues and signs as to how to solve all our problems are all around us; we just need to learn how to read those signs. Otherwise, life is like driving down a highway at night without our lights on. The signs are everywhere as we drive along – all there to guide and help us. But we need to raise our consciousness, which activates the light to see and read the signs.

"This isn't a sales pitch, Aryeh Lieb," I said and smiled. "Are you ready to test your reading skills?"

He smiled back. "Let's do it."

"Good. So, let's open The Book now so you can see where and how the third energy came about. The first Book of Moses, "At the Top" (Genesis), Chapter 22."

Verse 1:   And it came to pass after these things, that God tried Abraham, and said to him, 'Abraham,' and he said 'Here I am.'

Verse 2:   And He said, 'Please take your son, your only one whom have loved, [being] Isaac and go out to the Land of Moriah and **offer him up** as an "olah" [offering/a going up] on one of the mountains which I will tell you.

Verse 3: And Abraham got up early in the morning and bandaged his donkey and took his two young men and Isaac his son and split [**V-Y-V-K-A**] **wood/trees** of the offering and got up and went to the place where God told him.

Verse 4: On the third day Abraham lifted his eyes and saw the place from a distance.

Verse 5: And Abraham said to his young men, 'Sit yourselves here with the donkey and I and the young man will go until yonder and we will bow down and we will return to you.'

Verse 6: And Abraham took the **wood/trees** of the offering and put them **on** Isaac his son and he took **in** his hand the **fire** and the [slaughterer's] **knife** and they went the **two of them together**.

Verse 7: And Isaac said to Abraham his father and said, 'My father,' and he said, 'Here I am, son,' and he said, 'Here are the **fire** and the **wood/trees**, and where is the lamb for the offering?'

Verse 8: And Abraham said, 'God will show for Him the lamb for the offering, son.' And they went the **two of them together**.

Verse 9: And they came to the place where God told him and Abraham built there the alter and **arranged** the **wood/trees** and **bound** Isaac his son and placed him on the alter **from over** the **wood/trees**.

Verse 10: And Abraham sent out his hand and took the [slaughterer's] knife to slaughter [*lishchot*] his son.

Verse 11: And called to him an angel of God from the heavens and said, 'Abraham Abraham,' and he said, 'Here I am.'

Verse 12: And he said, 'Don't send out your hand to the young man and don't do anything to him because now I know that you are God-fearing and didn't spare your son your one from me.'

Verse 13:   And Abraham lifted up his eyes and saw…and took the
ram and raised it up as an offering **under** his son.

"Okay, now for starters, we need to remember three things at
the outset in order to understand what's going on here. First of all,
remember that Torah calls this the "Binding of Isaac" and not the
sacrifice of Isaac. You'll notice that God never said to sacrifice or
slaughter Isaac – it was never intended to be so; but rather, that was
Abraham's misunderstanding. In fact, the 'Trial of the Binding'
is called such – HaAkeda – because the word itself contains the
special meaning of Al Kiddushh Hashem, the Sanctification of
God's Name.[37]

"Think about it. The chapter opens with the give-away that
this was a trial, a spiritual test that God was putting to Abraham.
And Abraham's test was totally against any measure of logic. After
all, it was Abraham who all alone in the whole wide world was
going around telling people NOT to make human sacrifices. And
here everyone watched as he went off with tell-tale paraphernalia
to do exactly what he told the world not to do.[38]

"Two: Abraham is the chariot of Chesed, the attribute of
Mercy, which is the Right Column, whereas Isaac is the Chariot of
Gevurah, the attribute of Might, which is the Left Column; and,
when it comes to spirituality and metaphysics, positive energy
always needs to be before and a tad higher than the negative pole.
This is why Abraham fathered Isaac and why there are all these
seemingly redundant phrases like "Isaac his son" or "Abraham his
father." By stating it, it's basically like an activation of that energy
and a definition of its direction of flow.

The bottom-line goal of this entire passage is revealed from
the outset in verse 3, "V-Y-V-K-A" – the letters of Jacob's name,
Yaacov, i.e. the Chariot of the Central Column energy. And look

---

37   The Admor Yitzho Yehuda Yechiel Isaac of Kamarna's *Netiv Mitzvotecha*,
     part 1, p. 49.
38   See Rabbi Moshe Chaim Armoni's *Bati LeArmoni, Parashat "VaYare".*

at how this is accomplished. There is a crisscrossing of energies, while Abraham, the Right Column, always stays just above the Left. And this leads to the third point I want you to pay attention to. Notice that, Abraham (right) gives Isaac (left) the "wood/trees" (right), while Abraham (right) takes the fire and the knife (both left). Also notice the particular and deliberately unusual use of pronouns. The Right Column puts Right Column energy, the wood/trees, "on" Isaac (left), whereas Abraham (right) takes Left Column energy, the fire and knife, "in" to his hand. And then twice the Torah tells us that the two went "together" – that is, the Right Column bound the Left Column yet they were together.

Actually, there's a lot more going on here metaphysically and a number of spiritual goals were met. For example, the Kabbalah explains the phrases "arranged the wood/trees" and then that Isaac was placed "from over the wood/trees". The "trees" were The Tree of Life and The Tree of Knowledge of Good and Evil. He "arranged" them in such an order that the former was over the latter. Thus Abraham also corrected an aspect of Adam's sin here.[39]

There is also the point that the word donkey (Ch-M-R) refers to the material (Ch-M-R) aspect of this world. So it's significant that Abraham and Isaac left their donkey, i.e. the physical, material world, before proceeding up to Mount Moriah. Also noteworthy is that Isaac was actually placed on the altar, because the word altar (M-Z-B-Ch) is the acronym of the system of the Sefirot and in their order upward, from Malchut, through Ze'er Anpin, and Binah to Chochma. After all, the purpose was to raise Isaac, the attribute of Gevura, upward.

But, in addition to the metaphysical significance, there is also an important lesson gleaned on the simple, literal level here, and which the prophets (especially Jeremiah[40]) reiterate over and over, and that is: **God does not want us to sacrifice our children**. Period. We recite this passage every morning in *the Shacharit*

---

39 Ibid.
40 For example, see Jeremiah 19:5 and 32:35

prayer service; and it is called, as it has always been: The **Binding** of Isaac.

*

"So, tell me. This was the first time this new energy appeared in the world?"

"No. But it was the first time a mortal accessed it."

"Now what does that mean?! What else – Who else is there that did?!"

"God."

"Oh."

"It was how God created the universe. You see, until Abraham, those tzaddiks who possessed the divine wisdom were comprised of or held one attribute only. That's why they could not pass on their individual mode or path of serving God. Until Abraham.

"Abraham began a totally new path of devotion by way of alliance and integration of attributes, which he copied from the very method God used in creation. Each of the days of creation corresponds to the attributes of the Sefirot. The first attribute, the Sefira of Chesed (Mercy), corresponds with water; whereas the second attribute, the Sefira of Gevura (Might), corresponds with fire. And yet, on the first day God created light, which as fire, is of the second attribute, thus in terms of order should have come the second day. Then, on the second day, God created water. That is, the second day being vis-a-vis the second attribute, the Sefira of Gevura (Might), actually corresponds with fire; but God in essence crisscrossed the energies, thereby integrating together these two opposing forces: fire and water.[41]

*

Actually, we're discussing here two distinct spiritual concepts and achievements: Abraham's revolutionary work and the resulting Central Column energy. Abraham broke through the

---

41 Rabbi Moshe Chaim Armoni's *Bati LeArmoni, Parashat "Toldot"*, based on the *Zohar* II, 149b.

barrier between the upper and lower worlds; he was the first to do so and, in succeeding, opened the way for the whole world. What he effectedwas that the material aspect of the world would not impede the revelation of Light, of the spiritual, in this world. At this initial stage, just to maintain that the physical does not bother the spiritual, we see that Abraham 'bandaged' his donkey.[42] Abraham 'bandaged' or bound his donkey, meaning he subdued the material.

In this context, the next level, which is a higher path, is that where the physical body itself is purified – the body per se serves God and becomes a vessel for the Light. This level was effected and exemplified by Moses about whom it is written he put his wife and children to ride ON the donkey. And then the highest path and level of this framework is the ultimate goal, whereby the physical itself is holy. This is the meaning of the Messiah himself riding on a white donkey.[43]

The next occurrence of metaphysical energies mixing was by Moses. The laws of metaphysics decreed a separation between the upper worlds and the lower, as a result of the faulty and defying mixture done by Adam with the sin. So, before Revelation on Mount Sinai, because of Original Sin, the upper worlds would not come down to the lower one and the lower world would not go up – there was a total separation. As King David wrote 'The Heavens are for God, and the earth was given for man' (Psalms 115: 16).

But then at Revelation, Moses went up to God while God came down to Moses on Mount Sinai. And by this crisscrossing, the decree of separation was annulled. This effected the energy and opened the way to continue the revelation of the upper world into this world, and as such, being on a higher level, that from then on, the physical body itself could become holy.

"And they made for Me a Mishkan [Tabernacle] and Shachanti

---

42 Ibid, *parashat "Shmot"* page 15.
43 Ibid.

[I dwelled] inside them."[44]

The words Mishkan and Shahanti are both of the root of Shechina, being the revelation of God in the physical world.

What's also embedded in the Binding of Isaac section of Torah is a glimpse at the path of the journey. There is a distinct path laid out for us to use for our individual journey. God states: 'And you will remember the entire **way** which I your God led you this forty years in the desert.'[45] And then God tells Moses: 'Arise, go on the journey.'[46] Because, the way you journey matters too. And that's why the path is provided and defined too.

> And if the way be too great for you, because you cannot bear it, because it will be far from you the place that God choses to place His Name there because God your God will bless you.'[47]

I am an up-close God and not a God from afar.[48]

"Take a look at Abraham's big and final test. One of the hardest aspects of the trial was the illusion of God's distancing Himself from Abraham at the critical moment. Actually, that's why it was the test that it was: And Abraham went to the place where God told him to go. And then –

> On the **third** day, Abraham lifted his eyes and saw the Place from **afar**.[49]

See, that's where it stings. The Place, HaMakom, is another name for God. So, the action in this scene goes two ways, the

---

44   Exodus 25: 8.
45   Deuteronomy 8: 2.
46   Ibid, 10: 11.
47   Ibid, 14: 24.
48   Jeremiah 23:23.
49   Genesis 22: 4.

geographic 'place' and The Place. Both happen simultaneously. But my point here is to look at the conditions under which Abraham was tested, because they per se are part of the very test. God gives him the illusion that he's off all alone for three whole days, and that God was far and distant during those miserable three days. Isn't that the hardest part of hard times? – when you think you're all alone and that God is far away?

But that's precisely the test and precisely the illusion. For three days, Abraham was within this illusion that he was all alone. And even when those three days were up, he looked up and perceived God from afar, as if God was far off – far from him. Then, from within that illusion, was the test of what Abraham would do.

CHAPTER 13

I was just returning from my hour in the forest, approaching our clearing, when I caught sight of Dan Shimon talking. He was talking to the Creator. I stopped. Didn't want to alarm him or stop him. I was truly happy.

Just then, Aryeh Lieb appeared from behind the Fleet's wing farthest from the clearing, munching on a sandwich with a pickle carefully balanced between his pinkie and ring finger. This allowed his entire right hand to be free.

From the light streaming in from behind him, I could see crumbs fall when he bit from the one side of his hand, and pickle juice splurting when he bit from the other. "Dan Shimon, what are you doing?!" he asked with his mouth still half full. I could see Dan Shimon struggle not to be distracted. He raised his finger signaling Aryeh Lieb to wait.

"One!" Aryeh Lieb announced. Dan Shimon then drew a spiral in the air trying to signal Aryeh Lieb to wait to bug him a bit later.

"Oh, it's a movie!" Aryeh Lieb concluded. "Great. Charades. I'm game!" And with this, Dan Shimon completely turned his back on Aryeh Lieb to try to regain his concentration and tune out the distraction.

"Back. A movie that starts with the word 'back'. Hmm." There was silence for the next few moments as Aryeh Lieb munched and thought. Dan Shimon's back was still turned.

"Actually," Aryeh Lieb said to Dan Shimon, "I'm not that up on movies. I give up. What movie starts with 'back'?" Aryeh Lieb called out. Silence. "Dan Shimon, I give up!" he repeated.

Dan Shimon twirled around annoyed. "Would you cut that out! I'm not playing any charades."

"Well, what were you doing?" I continued to hear Aryeh Lieb ask. And I concluded that that was my sign to proceed.

"Another old couple's spat?" I half laughed. Dan Shimon shot me a look with the sides of his mouth tightly raised, "Oh please!"

"DAN SHIMON, WHAT WERE YOU DOING????" Aryeh Lieb didn't let up.

Dan Shimon looked at me and asked, "Should I tell him?"

"Tell him what?!" Aryeh Lieb repeated Dan Shimon's words as he came over, totally serious by now.

"By all means," I said. "Reveal the secret to him. That's why I'm here."

"What? What? What?" is all Aryeh Lieb could say out of his curiosity. He looked at the two of us, his head slightly forward. "What SECRET?!"

Just then a pick-up truck screeched as it pulled onto the dirt road leading to our clearing, leaving a wake of flying dust behind it. It barely came to a full stop beside us when three very energetic boys bounced out and raced to the planes. "I want to go in this one," one pointed. "And, grandpa, I want to fly in that one," another announced out of breath.

"Okay. Okay, calm down boys. I told you, you'd all get to go. Take it easy." The proud grandfather was a large but fit farmer with a well-worn red plaid shirt, denim overalls and salt-and-pepper hair.

The oldest and youngest grandchildren were assigned to be together in Dan Shimon's two-passenger Travel Air. The youngest was much younger than the two older brothers who were evidently very close in age. The middle brother would fly in Aryeh Lieb's one-passenger Fleet.

The preparations were part of the fun for the youngsters, who eagerly donned the helmets and climbed into their seats. The two pilots fastened everybody's seat belts. And we all watched the propellers set in motion, which eventually gave the magical illusion of being invisible, except for a faint blur. They were spinning so fast, you could see the trees and field on their other side, right through them.

Once they were all off the ground, the grandfather came over. I showed him one of our reclining spots on the ground, and he accepted, leaning on the improvised table-arm rest – that one and only flat-topped rock on the side of our clearing.

"It's nice of you boys to offer such fun for so fair a price," he began.

"Well, actually, it's only them," I confessed. "I don't fly." He looked around I assume to verify there were no other aircraft.

"Times are a bit difficult," he commented. "I don't quite know what to do. It's hard to find good, clean activities to occupy the grandkids with over the entire summer without costing an arm and a leg." I nodded in sympathy.

"You should tell Him all about it," I proposed. He looked at me with knitted brows. "Your friends at best can empathize and sympathize, but your only real address for help is upward. Give Him an earful, and in full detail."

"Son, I'm already a believer," he said in a tone revealing a tad of insult.

"Oh, I believe you," I assured him.

"Deep down in my heart, I know He's the only one running the show. I go once a week to prayer services. For sure, I believe," the farmer said.

"Belief is such a big thing," I began, "that for sure you should keep it deep down in your heart; but you should also bring it out as part of your everyday living. Bring it up into the open and use it daily.

"He's not just there for a communal weekly prayer service.

He's with us right now, right here, watching and listening to us. Sometimes we realize this. But it's the most important thing to remember and internalize and live with all the time." He considered me, but listened intently.

"Consider your recent hardships. Most of the time, our hardships are sent to us to cause or force us to stop, catch our bearings, gain perspective and focus. When all is good and running well, we keep ourselves on autopilot – a constant flow of activities that entertain us and distract us from the mundane. Sometimes it's only when things get tough that we realize that when the party was over, we weren't left with anything substantial.

"The constant bombardment of stimuli on our senses doesn't allow or leave any room for us to concentrate, reflect and consider what's real. Where we're really going. Sometimes times get hard to force us to look upward and establish a better and different relationship with Him.

"With tests, one either goes up or down. So, why not make the choice to choose to go up – to grow and rise from the situation. And that smacks right at the essence of our free will." He looked down and just kept nodding. "Don't despair, my friend," I told the farmer, "you'll see that things'll get better soon."

"Everything in all creation happens for a reason. And as hard as it is at first, we have to believe that everything that happens is good and really for the best. It wouldn't be called a trial if it weren't trying. Sometimes, I'd even say most times, these trials are to get us to open up and create a receptacle of ourselves for the good to come in. When you speak to Him, your spoken word creates a vessel for receiving. And that's why I told you to bring your belief out from deep down in your heart."

"Well, I don't know," the farmer said.

"Consider your problem a message sent from above asking you to call. He wants to hear from you, hear your voice spoken out loud."

"How would I go about making that call," he said with a smile.

"Just talk," I answered. "With pure simplicity, just talk as if you were talking to a friend, which He is – Father and friend. And just as with any other friend, the more you talk, the closer you'll become, and, in turn, the more that friend will be on your mind. It builds."

"What, just talk to the air?"

"I guess it may look like that, but it's not."

"Well, I don't know. What if my wife sees me talking what looks like to the air? Then what? She'll start to question my state of mind. Heck, that's all I need," he said with a light chuckle. I smiled too.

"You can either choose to talk in a solitary place, a room, back yard, wherever. In fact, they say it's best to go outside, alone into a field or grove among the trees and include nature. Second place would be to go to a solitary spot in your house. And third place, but still good would be in semi-hiding," I said with a wide smile. "Even under your covers in bed or faking a phone call. Actually it's not so fake, because you are making a call somewhat. You could just talk into the receiver. Whatever works best for you." I saw him consider all that. He raised his brows.

"Or," I continued with emphasis, "and even better yet...or maybe in addition...reveal the secret to your wife too." He looked up at me with surprise.

"You'll see, it'll make you feel good too – get a load off. But don't get me wrong. I'm not talking here about some kind of psychological exercise. No. This will truly help you. It's like plugging in to an electrical socket. It hooks you up. It conducts energy. It's real and it works."

"Oh, I guess I could give it a try."

"Good. I really wish the best to you."

"Thanks.

The Travel Air and Fleet came into sight and caught our attention. They flew a nice formation together. And as they came closer, we could see the boys in both planes waving to each other.

We could feel the excitement of the boys as they landed. Sure enough, they started their rendition while still on board. One called over from still inside, "Grandpa, it was great!"

"Grandpa," another yelled over, "you gotta go. It's so cool. We'll be happy to wait for you."

"Yeah, you should try it too," the third and youngest quipped.

"Oh now, boys, that's quite okay," the proud grandfather replied. "I actually got more than I bargained for in coming." And with that he looked at me and smiled a warm and fatherly smile. "Thank you for all your good advice."

"You're welcome," I responded. "Come by whenever you like."

"I sure will." And with that he turned with his grandkids for his truck.

* * *

As the nice farmer was leaving with his grandchildren, a couple of cars pulled up. A line formed for flights, and Aryeh Lieb and Dan Shimon flew back-to-back flights close to sunset. Since people were waiting and mingling in the clearing for their turn, I decided that was my cue. That time of day to take stock, introspection and self-judgment. After all, if one judges himself down here, then they won't judge him up there.

To be alone with the Creator Himself. I walked away from the clearing and into the forest that bordered the one side of the field.

"Abba, father," I began, "thank you so much for letting me talk to that good farmer, for giving me the opportunity to try to help him. At least it seemed to have helped, as he implied from his remark as he was leaving. I just fear that I might have insulted him for that moment then. I tried to explain after that and redress the hurt. And I think he forgave me. You too, Abba, please forgive me. I truly did not intend to insult or be condescending. You, of course, know that.

"Oh dear and compassionate Father, please let me continue to be your loyal messenger. And please help that good soul. Let him feel Your presence. And open the Gate of Livelihood for him.

Please also let me feel your presence and draw closer to You. Abba, keep me with You. I want only You.

Oh, and Abba, please let even that farmer's wife and grandchildren feel your presence and open up to talk to and draw closer to You. The grandfather was concerned, so please keep his grandkids on the right path. Let them succeed and bring pride and happiness to their grandparents."

I was out there about an hour and poured my heart out. I discussed all the issues of the day and now I felt a tremendous lightness, the sweetness of relief, in knowing all's well. Everything was now in good and proper hands.

Name

CHAPTER 14

Aryeh Lieb needed to go get gas for his Fleet. I decided to tag along. I'd take one of the jerry-cans and at the same time put in a bit of maintenance on the case I was given in deposit for my soul. In other words, I thought I'd get out a bit and get some exercise for my body.

Just near the gas station was a small fair the county put together. Old fashioned ferris wheel, carousel, cotton candy, and clowns. I jabbed my elbow lightly in Aryeh Lieb's side, "Let's go," I said, my chin somewhat pointing to the fair.

"What?!" Aryeh Lieb was thrown off. "What are you going to do, take my hand and buy me a lollipop?"

"Didn't your mommy ever tell you candy is bad for your teeth? And, you're a big boy, Aryeh Lieb. But if you insist, I guess I could hold your hand. But let's go." He smiled, as I did back.

"You're serious."

"Yeah."

"Why?"

"Let's say to whet our bionic vision," I replied.

"What?!" After all, 'The Six Million Dollar Man' was over along time ago. We left our cans with a good natured guy running a cold drinks booth.

"Let's take an exercise in looking through matter and seeing the inner intelligence," I said. Now he gave me an interested look.

A young elementary school aged boy walked by next to his parents proudly holding a wand of cotton candy. "Amazing what you can do with a meager tablespoon of common sugar," I commented. "And do you know how much a tablespoon of sugar costs?" I added when I saw the price list.

"Yeah, but the candy is all nice and fluffed up," Aryeh Lieb took their defense.

"With air."

"Yeah. With air."

"And do you know how much air costs?"

"I see," he said amused.

"Aryeh Lieb, have you ever seen one of those diagrams of an atom?"

"Sure. You've got the nucleus core with protons, and orbiting around it are electrons," he began rattling off from familiarity. I, in response, pulled out my modern-day genie from my pocket. But instead of rubbing the lamp to make my wish, I typed in my wish to Google for the familiar diagram. And, as fast as I could say poof, there it was – granted, and in color.

"Okay, now," I said, "take a look at the atom. What do you see?"

"You mean the structure of the atom we learned in school, like I just said?"

"I'm asking you to tell me what you see. Here, take a look, right here."

"Well, I see a nucleus and electrons orbiting around, and –" he recited.

"No," I cut him off. "That's what you've been taught to see. Now, again, take a good look. What do you see? What do you really see?"

"Umm. I don't know. Protons. The lines of the orbiting –"

Illusions. They are not only optical ones. Sometimes they are one thing, perfectly clear to the naked eye one way, but we've been so deeply inculcated that what we see is totally different, we lose touch with what's really real. In fact, until only very recently (if you look at the grand scale of human existence), if you questioned authority, even politely, on what was obvious but not acceptable, you would easily have been burned at the stake by the church or had hemlock poured down your throat.

The late comedian Robin Williams had hilarious skits where he pointed out exactly how absurd it was that Hollywood, in picking the cast to play ancient Romans and Greeks, always chose actors with strong British accents. In fact, especially the role of emperor had to be played with a good Heightened RP. And, of course, we've come to expect this and associate Romans with prim and proper English accents, as in 'Oh, I do say, dear Caesar...' when clearly Julius, an Italian, should have been speaking more along the lines of , 'Yo! Hey ya Tony, whatcha do dat fo'?!'

Similarly, to date, as I've already noted, when we imagine King David and his royal palace, we automatically conjure up Shakespearean scenes like something out of Hamlet or Macbeth. Though clearly, King David was nowhere close to being European. That's part of the illusion. The disillusion is that his great-grandmother, Ruth, was not a white-gloved, parlor-sitting Lady, but a Moabite Arab woman from Trans-Jordan who converted to Judaism.

"No," I finally had to set him straight. "Let's go back. Think what it is these atoms represent. What are they?"

"The building blocks of physical matter."

"Good. It's what makes up what we call 'solid matter', right?"

"Yes."

"And the electrons orbit on an invisible yet set course."

"Correct."

"Okay. So now look again. I'm really asking about what should be dead-ringer obvious. Just how 'solid' are these building blocks? How much of the atom is actually really made of solid matter? The nucleus is really only a tiny fraction of the atom's overall volume, but is most of its mass. That is, the vast majority of the very basic building block of physical matter isn't even 'solid' or even physical matter. If you really look, then you'll see that that's precisely the illusion: That the building blocks of 'solid' physical matter are not really that at all. Rather, it's mostly made of empty space," I summed up. "And that's the disillusion."

"But, it's not like I can put my arm through a solid brick wall."

"No. You can't. But notice what you just said. Solid to us is something that's totally physical material. Right?"

"I guess you could say that," Aryeh Lieb agreed.

"And yet, it really only gives the illusion of solid matter."

"What does?"

"Things. Anything. Everything's made of atoms, no? Because everything is made of atoms, and atoms are primarily comprised of empty space, what we think of as 'solid' isn't what we thought solid meant. God permeates creation from inside and out under the camouflage of what we call air or empty space.

"Actually, it's more than that. What keeps the atom together is the balance of its metaphysical force. And, therefore, what really keeps our hand from going through a brick wall is not its infinitesimal physicality, but the almost-100% of its internal-metaphysical energy. And that is the illusion of the physical world.

"I might even take this a step further and note that it doesn't take much physical matter to cause a big explosion: The weight of matter converted to energy in the bomb that destroyed the city of Hiroshima was less than one ounce. [50] This is because what causes the energy is the disruption of the metaphysical balance.

"Oh."

"Just like the cotton candy."

"Is that what you think of when you see cotton candy?" he asked me.

"Aryeh Lieb," I began, "the Creator is constantly sending us messages. The question is only whether or not we pick up on them. We talk in words to Him, and sometimes this is how He answers us. Don't look for UFOs and meteors. Everything has a

---

50 Stephen Hawking's *A Briefer History of Time*, chapter 5, p. 35.

meaning and a purpose. Observe all the details, big and small, of this big, wonderful world.

"Take the empty space we talked about – air. Do you know what air is?"

"Oxygen and –"

"No. Leave the illusion side alone. What is it really, on the metaphysical, root level? To find out, you always need to look at the word for that in the language of God's Word, in the Holy Tongue, in Hebrew. And in Hebrew, air is 'avir' – A-V-Y-R – which are the letters of Ohr (A-V-R), Light, plus Y, being 10. Air is the Light of God, Ohr, through His ten Sefirot. All of what we see as empty space, all around us and in the atom, all of it is God's Light. We don't even understand what we're really saying when we say things like, it's just air."

"Light."

"The Endless Light. That means that air is the physical expression of the Light of the Ten Sefirot. It's all around us and inside of us, in our lungs and in each and every cell. So, God is everywhere. And that's in or through a physical means."

"Air."

"Exactly. And remember when I told you what the purpose of existence is in a nutshell?"

"Yes."

"Well, to rephrase it, it's to reveal and recognize God in the thick of the illusive, physical world. That's what's called revealing the Shechina: The manifestation of God in, within, and from within the physical world. So, this is what we're doing by looking at air from this perspective. Because Science and Torah are really two sides of the same coin. Science deals with and explains HOW the world works, whereas Torah gives the WHY.

"We need to back up a second, though, to check out the orbit paths. Take a look at the diagram. You see those lines for the orbit of the electrons?"

"Yes."

"They're an illusion. They don't exist. That is, the orbit lines don't exist. People had to draw them on to show us the pattern and structure. But in reality, there are no lines. Not for atoms, not for planets and moons around mother planets or the sun. The lines are drawn to help us understand the order.

"But, you know, it's all like a puppeteer who is recognized for his art and level of professionalism by how well he can hide the strings to his puppets. And the best is when you can't even see the strings at all. Think about it. What makes all those orbiting things orbit? What is their internal, built-in GPS that tells them just how, where, and how fast to journey? The answer is in the empty space. That very empty space that is the illusion, because it's really God. And who's the master puppeteer? The One pulling all the strings that we don't see – God.

"You might also say that this two-sided coin is really part of the three-pronged illusion. One, we appear as separate beings. The disillusion is that all of our souls are part of one whole. The second prong is that, like air everywhere, there is only God; and everything is an expression of Him. It may not look that way, but looks give an optical illusion. And, three, solid matter is almost completely made up of God's Light. That is, physical matter is mostly spiritual matter. And here air gives us a good example of how that's applied."

"Even cotton candy."

"There you go. Even cotton candy," I agreed. And with that Aryeh Lieb wanted a few moments to think. We continued to walk about just taking in the sounds.

"Did you bring that bottle of yours?" he broke the silence between us.

"Of course," I answered. "Always." And I pulled it out of my backpack and handed it to him. He pulled what was waiting for him.

> *Know, that one must always focus on the inner*
> *intelligence of every matter, and bind himself to the*
> *wisdom and inner intelligence that is to be found*
> *in each thing. This, so that the intelligence which*
> *is in each thing may enlighten him, that he may*
> *draw closer to God through that thing. For the inner*
> *intelligence is a great light that shines for a person in*
> *all his ways.*
> *The Writings of Rabbi Nachman of Breslev*
> *("Likutei Moharan") Part I, section 1.*

"Hey, I already got this one before," Aryeh Lieb exclaimed.

"Well then it must be relevant again and maybe with new light," I answered. "That is part of the secret of the cycle of the year and rereading the Torah, parsha by parsha, again and again. The cycle should be an ever-climbing spiral. Each time you reread, you should see it on a higher level."

Then another note popped up from the bottle as we continued walking. It said –

> *There's a certain box from inside which science still*
> *thinks and thus requires certain plugs to patch up*
> *what doesn't make sense by its terms – plugs and*
> *patches so that reality fits nicely into scientific theory.*
> *This is where the necessity for concepts like ether and*
> *the antigravity force, the cosmological constant, and*
> *supergravity arose. And all have been knocked on*
> *their heads. The string theories too don't cooperate*
> *with reality, as they are 'consistent only if space-*
> *time has either ten [the ten Sefirot] or twenty-six*
> *[gematria for the Tetragrammaton] dimensions,*
> *instead of the usual four.'* [51]

---

51 Hawking's *A Briefer History of Time*, chapter 11, p.128; my add-ons in the brackets.

We strolled about some more and came to the carousel. There was the typical bustle and din around in the background. Children of different ages were on the horses. A mother was up holding her very young daughter, helping her hold on. "Now I can do it myself," came a little voice to her mother.

"Well, okay, sweetheart. Go ahead." And she got off, but continued to keep watch. All was well until the little girl's horse was on the farthest side of her mother. The center part of the carousel blocked their eye contact.

"Mommy!" came an instant cry.

"It's okay. I'm right here. I'm right here, honey." And as the horse continued around and they could see each other, all was well. But again, at that precise moment, and it was really only a split second, when she could not actually see her mother, the little girl got scared and cried "Mommy!"

"Isn't that just like us?" I began. Aryeh Lieb looked at me puzzled. "The Creator is always with us, always watching us. We go about our lives and at certain points think that He doesn't see us anymore. And, of course, unlike that mother, He can see right through solid matter. But it just looks like we're far away and out of sight. Some then get scared. Others may think they can then do all kinds of things, just by mistakenly perceiving that 'nobody's watching.' Of course, that's part of the illusion." I concluded.

We kept walking. I pointed to the great ferris wheel looming high over the fairgrounds. "Your turn now, "I said to Aryeh Lieb. "What do you see?"

A brother and sister were sitting together on one of the seats. He wore a camouflage shorts set and she had a high pony tail. They were just beginning their ascent. The boy started jumping in his seat. When they got to the top, he spread his arms wide and then up, as if he had just broken the tape at the race finish line. He then began to calm down as his segment went over the top and began its descent.

"That really is like the way of the world," Aryeh Lieb began.

"Power and glory come and go. No one stays on top forever." He looked at me for approval and I nodded for him to continue. "It's amazing, though, how few of those running for the top realize this. They show off all kinds of satisfied signs of victory at that moment that they hit the top as if they're sure they'll be there forever. I guess it's also a kind of test: How do you act when you're given 'your' moment of fame and glory? How do you look and how do you use your new powers – use them or abuse them or just show off?

"And the one who keeps descending lower and lower needs to bear in mind that most of the time, just when you think you've hit rock bottom, and maybe you really have, that is precisely the point at which you stop going down and start seeing yourself go up," he concluded and looked at me askingly.

"Very good," I said. And we both smiled. "Just one more point," I noted. "And, I believe the most important..." I began.

"I know," Aryeh Lieb cut me off. "Let me say it. Self-check: Do you know who's running the wheel? There is really no such thing as a 'self-made man.' That's idolatry. You have to act in understanding that you are being raised and not that you are raising yourself."

"Very good," I acknowledged, much like a teacher grading a student. "Now we can start heading back." He looked at me and I could sense his satisfaction. We looked at each other and smiled.

"Okay," he said as his smile widened, "I'll forgo the lollipop."

CHAPTER 15

"Tell me something. I've got a question for you, a million dollar question."

"Sounds good. Let's hear it."

"Going back to the Garden of Eden before the sin and the eating from the Tree of Knowledge of Good and Evil when everything was perfect and paradise."

"Okay."

"What's a snake doing in paradise? How can there be, quite literally, a snake in the grass in such a place?"

"Nice. Great question. How about if I add to that another related question, since we're taking things here to the next level, and that is 'Why was Eve punished with childbearing?' Adam's punishment directly relates to his sin of eating from the forbidden fruit, as the snake's punishment of eating dust also relates directly to tempting forbidden eating. But what does Eve's punishment have to do with eating? Have you ever thought about that?"

"Alright. Good point. Does anybody anywhere talk about this?"

"In the sea of wisdom – tons. Our Sages discuss both these very questions, over centuries, even millennia.

"So, let's go way way back to the beginning, and even before that. The Written Torah tells the complete story of This World, this time only, from its beginning to its end. It begins 'Beresheet' – with the second Hebrew letter 'bet' which, in the structure of the letter itself, has a wall to what comes before it to its right. Remember that Hebrew goes from right to left. The letter 'bet' opens only to the left. The Oral Torah, on the other hand, expands and tells what happened before 'At the beginning' or 'At the top'.

"The Talmud tells us[52] that there were 974 generations that were 'crumpled up' to be created before the creation of our world, but were not created. That is, these shards never actually, materially existed. Instead, God took the souls of these 974 generations and planted them, sort of sprinkled them, throughout all of the generations of our world, because these pre-primordial souls are immense and powerful. Too powerful, that is.

"These souls are so strong that they can quite literally destroy the world. More specifically, these are the souls of the pre-creation World of Chaos. They have the power only to destroy but not to build. We see these souls in every generation in the power leaders and tyrants of the world: Stalin, Hitler, etc.

"So, God basically uses them up by only planting a few each time, in each generation; and they will continue to reincarnate until the arrival of the Mashiach. King David teaches us in his Psalms that God 'remembered His covenant forever, the word which He has commanded to the thousandth generation' (105: 8). And you'll notice that Moses is the 26th generation after Adam. So, add the 974 generations that preceded the creation of our world and the 26 until Moses, and you get exactly 1000 generations to receiving the Torah, the covenant.

"Now, I want to go back again and explain that our world was created from the shards of the previous Worlds of Chaos. We learn this from the opening verses of the Torah: 'And the earth was chaos and darkness...' (Genesis 1: 2), emphasis being on the word

---

52   Tractate Chagigah 13b-14a and Tractate Zevachim 116a. Rabbi Moshe Chaim Armoni explains this in his *Bati LeArmoni, parashat "Ki Tetze"*, pages 268-269.

'was'. That is, the world already 'was' – already existed."[53]

"Whoa, that's a lot of meaning packed into that teeny tiny singular word."

"Don't let the size fool you. Midrash Rabba Shmot 2: 4 explains that this quote-un-quote 'little' word, 'haya', signifies that something is 'metukan lekach' – made to do something special: Adam WAS set to die; the snake WAS set for tribulation; Noah WAS set for redemption; ditto for Moses; Yosef WAS set for livelihood; Mordechai WAS set to save.[54] So the shards of the last worlds were set to create our world.

"Just don't forget that these 974 generations precede our world and thus also precede the very existence of time. Fortunately for us in our generation, today we have the cognitive faculties and tools to grasp this: Cyber- "existence" or virtual- "reality" – that are all time and space free.

"Basically, all of those previous worlds and cycles and sabbaticals that are mentioned are all part of a single cache of virtual blueprints. And, just as the prototype design on a hi-tec computer 'feels' real and is scaled and detailed to give the 'illusion' of depth and reality, and is even 'real' on the computer, nevertheless, it is not 'really' in and of the material, physical world."

"Wait. So it says that there were pre-existing worlds?"

"Yes. The Torah, in the Zohar and Midrash discuss this. There was a pre-existing time order. God built worlds and then destroyed them. But they did not exist in a context of time. Rabbi Shimon Bar Yochai describes them like the sparks that fly up from a blacksmith's anvil – they spark for a split moment only. And then they disappear, because they have no real existence.[55] Think how you use the delete button on your computer, where, with the

---

53 *Zohar* part I, section 16 and *Midrash Bresheet Rabba* 1: 5 and explained in Rabbi Moshe Chaim Armoni's *Bati LeArmoni, parashat "Beresheet"*, page 1.
54 – *Bati LeArmoni, parashat "Bo"*, page 85.
55 *Galei Amikta*, page 63 – – written by Spain's Jewish Golden Age Kabbalist Rabbi Yosef Al-Kastile, edited by his descendant Rabbi Moshe Chaim Armoni.

slightest press of that button, all of the detailed, realistic-looking, cyber-space real, virtual blueprints can disappear. And that's pretty much how it was.

"See, the illusion is that these 974 generations actually existed, the illusionary word here being 'actually'. The disillusion is that they all existed as *potential* blueprints that got crumpled up and trashed and never *actually* got launched into reality. Note that crumpled up within the balled up rejects were also the time-space that accompanied and incorporated these generations. That is, the illusion is of the existence of their time and space. They really did exist; but they did so in potential only, never in actuality, which is the disillusion. If you've ever seen a blueprint, then you'll understand how in the drawing – of what can potentially exist – they show the landscape around the building, and even show people too, to provide scale and a better illusion of reality. It's all there in the blueprint – all there, and in precise detail, but in potential only.

"Okay, so Adam's world in Eden was basically a composite of all these immense raw energies or souls reformed from the shards of what came before and was destroyed. The snake comprised all of the evil of the pre-existing Worlds of Chaos. There was no evil in Adam or in the Garden – all was concentrated in that arch-snake.[56] That is also to say that before Adam's sin, evil was seen as a mere illusion."[57]

"Illusion?"

"Yes: Illusion. And, just as the worlds that comprised the snake did not have physical expression, if Adam and Eve had not ingested this poisonous energy of mish-mash, being the 'forbidden fruit', then good and evil would have remained separate and separated elements in our world. Evil would have only existed outside of man and not within him, as the Evil Inclination.[58]

*

56 Rabbi Moshe Chaim Armoni's *Bati LeArmoni, parashat "Beresheet"* page 2.
57 Strive For Truth, part 5, parashat "VaYeshev", p. 155.
58 *Galei Amikta*, page 67.

In his article "Adam's Test and Its Lesson For Us", Rabbi Dessler quotes the Rav Chaim of Volozhyn in the latter's "Nefesh HaChaim":

> "Before the sin, Adam was obviously free to go in any direction he wished – toward good or toward the opposite. This was, after all, the purpose of all creation; moreover, we see that he did, in fact, sin. However, the desire for evil was not inside him. Internally, he was completely good… without any admixture of evil or any inclination towards it. The desire for evil stood apart from him, outside him; he was free to make it part of himself if he wished, just as a person is free to walk into fire. The incitement to sin had to come from outside him – from the 'serpent.' This is very different from our present circumstances, where the *yetzer* which tempts a person to sin is within the person himself, and it seems to him that he himself wants to sin, not that someone outside him is persuading him"
>
> (Nefesh HaChaim 1: 6).[59]

> "In Adam before the sin, the roles were reversed. He was created with an undeviating nature [per Kohelet/ Ecclesiastes 7: 29], without any inclination to evil. Adam's 'I' desired only the good. So, in what form could sin attract him? Only if it came to him from the outside saying, 'You ought to do this.' The temptation had to take the form of an invitation to do a mitzvah."[60]

Adam's "test was not choosing between good and evil as we understand them, but between two kinds of good…[N]ot to eat from the tree of knowledge of

---

59 *Strive For Truth!* Part 5 by Rabbi Eliyahu E. Dessler, English by Rabbi Aryeh Carmell, parashat Beresheet, pages 12-13.
60 Rav Dessler, ibid, page 13.

good and evil…meant that he was not to lower himself to the level of knowing good and evil as realities… [Adam] had been placed in *Gan Eden* without any direct contact with evil. He believed that if he lowered his *madrega* [level] a little and allowed evil – to a small extent – to enter him, and then conquered the evil for the greater glory of God – the resulting Kiddush Hashem would be incomparably greater. He would be transforming darkness itself into light!"[61]

*

"After the Worlds of Chaos that is the essence from which the snake came, if you take a good look at what evil is, you'll see that it's a mishmash of good and evil, exactly what the snake was. And at this deeper level of understanding, we redefine evil as essentially displaced good. Evil is something or an aspect of someone that is per se good, but not done or undertaken in the appropriate time, manner, and/or place. It could mean the wrong recipient or person or thing, or improper or wrong timing. And, manner would include degree or quantity too. Evil takes things to such extremes and out of context and proportion that you can't see the good at the core. Thus it also blocks our ability to discern God's goodness, His totality of goodness.

"But while evil may be displaced good, never underestimate the difference. Evil is evil, bad is bad, wrong is wrong. And doing wrong is wrong and matters. Mixing up good and evil is our biggest problem – it's the root cause of all our problems. Even on a most basic, seemingly insignificant level, we see this mix up all the time: People today wear their underwear on the outside – under and out are mixed up. People display what should be private, publicly. In this way, everything is backward, topsy-turvy, up-side-down. But you know what? – it's off just 'slightly'. Remember the story

---

61 Ibid, pages 14-15.

of the Garden? Just a slight adjustment is all it takes to put things in proper order and proportion – in their rightful place, to make them right and good.

"This resonates with that underlying essence motif of this world that everything needed to complete tikkun is already here and is good – but that good is just a little off and needs fine-tuning."

"So anything can be made good?"

"No. Not now that good and evil have been all mixed together. I'll give you an example. Take, for instance, meat. Is it a sin to eat meat?"

"Depends."

"Right. You can shecht and salt and bless with all the meditative kavanot of the Rashash, but if the meat is from pig, we have no way to do tikkun on pork, and thus it's a sin. And thus it remains among those things that cannot be made good. The physical aspect is very significant and instrumental, whereas before the sin there was no physicality. So, those animals not possessing the physical signs delineated in the Torah that indicate that metaphysically they can have us do tikkun for them, are totally off limits: treif. There's nothing we can do to do tikkun for them. Therefore, the commandment regarding them is abstinence – as in the "Do not" commandments.

"Okay, so, what Adam wanted to do was to complete the tikkun of that aspect of Good in the Tree of Knowledge of Good and Evil and bind it with the Tree of Life[62], a feat that would have been possible had he waited for Shabbat to set in. And this is where we slowly come to see that additional piece of the puzzle – the meaning of Eve's punishment.

"The snake constituted the sparks, souls, of all the evil of those 974 generations; and just as evil does in this world, the snake worked in two ways. One: To keep the good from achieving tikkun within this world – with constructive and positive actions. And, two: To keep us from the mitzvoth (the 1st means), by steering

---

62 Ibid, *parashat "Toldot"*, page 126.

us away to deal with that part of creation for which we mortals cannot do tikkun. If we're busy with the 2nd means, then we won't be able to do mitzvoth (the 1st).

"That is, the snake's strategy comes in a 2-flavored, 2-pronged direction: either a frontal attempt to pull us away from the Tree of Life, or, an indirect one by engaging us in spiritual work that is of the Tree of Knowledge of Good and Evil, as in 'Do it for the sake of, or in the name of, doing a mitzvah.'

"Let's remember, Adam was the composite of all of the sparks of creation that were capable of tikkun, of being corrected by himself and Eve together – the 'good'. All of the sparks that Adam could not correct, the 'evil', were what comprised the snake. The tikkun or correction of the good sparks in Adam would be by being fruitful and multiplying – bringing about the good into this world. Thus, the very first commandment is exactly that: to have children.

"The temptation was the snake's selling Eve the 'snake-oil' story that she could correct and raise the sparks within the snake. But, like pork, Eve did not have the kelim, the spiritual faculties, by which to do that. From here, by Eve taking from the snake, she brought evil into herself, making it a part of herself from within. She thought she would be able to correct these sparks of evil by being born from her. But she was wrong. And, therefore, her punishment was in the same area – childbearing.

> The Son of David [Mashiach] will not come until all of
> the souls will have been included in bodies
>
> (Tractate Niddah 13b).

A very distinct number of souls need to come down to this world in order for this world to achieve tikkun. This is why the whole issue of childbearing is at the forefront in the spiritual warfare of the Erev Rav against the Nation of Israel. Several million abortions have already taken place since the founding of the State of Israel. It is, quite literally, a battle over the human womb, the fight of the snake, because with every child born, we get that much closer to finalizing the correction of all of the correctable sparks from Adam.

"The snake tried to sell Eve the notion that she could be like God and that by internalizing them, she could handle the evil sparks just as she can the good ones. But here's the clincher: With all our spiritual and mental abilities and potential by way of our free will, we mortals just ain't God. Like it or not, we do not have the power to handle those sparks of evil. We are not God. And it is this truth that the snake twisted.

"And I'll also add that anything or anyone who tries to keep us from the mitzvoth, being the Tree of Life, becomes a vehicle or embodiment of the snake itself. Similarly, and what connects with Adam's punishment, is the point that the mitzvoth, the Tree of Life, are themselves part of the reward – they are the connection to the Garden of Eden. To lose the mitzvoth, by choosing instead the Tree of Knowledge of Good and Evil, that in itself is the punishment – by doing so, we lose the Garden of Eden."

"Let me see if I got it. To spell out the deceit, the snake was basically correct in saying that if Adam and Eve were able to convert the souls of the 974 generations to good, that is, succeeding in doing their tikkun, then they would in fact be like God. But, that is just it – that was the half-truth bait – if we were able. The covered up part of the whole truth is that we mortals do not have God's capabilities, and thus cannot do that tikkun, or be God."

"Exactly.

"Okay, so all evil was concentrated in the snake outside of Adam and Eve and then later became de-concentrated and a part placed inside them as the Evil Inclination?"

"Yes. That's pretty much it. Though it's more than just a feature that exists. Its expression is when we don't have the 'kelim' to deal with it. That is, the Yetzer is like a nagging fly. It doesn't fully express itself when you're standing there with a rolled-up newspaper all ready to swat it. No. Like the snake, it knows just when to strike. So with our analogy, the Evil Inclination is like a fly buzzing madly around in the car when you're going over 100 kph on a busy highway."

"Yeah, I see what you mean. You could go berserk trying to keep up defensive driving."

"What we need the most defense from is the yetzer."

"Right again."

*

"But now I want to refocus on the concept of shards. The fact that God created our world from the recycled shards of potential past worlds set a precedent that enables us too to recreate a new world from a discarded past. It's called repentance, teshuva. And the root source of repentance is precisely in this central concept and study of Torah, regarding the 974 generations. From this root is our ability to go back in time and change history, putting ourselves on a new and fresh line of cause and effect, and thus a new present and future.

The wormhole that science is looking for? This is it. Repentance is the wormhole – the ability to recycle past shards and take a short cut into a new reality.

CHAPTER 16

After discussing "The Arrow of Time" in his first book, in chapter 9 of *A Brief History of Time*, in his *A Briefer History of Time*, Dr. Stephen Hawking devotes his entire chapter 10 to "Wormholes and Time Travel". I have to be honest, it sounds a bit like they're really just gaming with equations (e.g. Kurt Godel's) that would make it "possible to get back to earth before you set out...time travel implies faster-than-light travel"[63]; but, alas, science cannot break the speed-of-light barrier[64] even with only elementary particles in particle accelerators. Thus, they have to "rule out both rapid space travel and travel back in time"[65]. And despite all this, it does not look like they can even strive with all their equations-playing to get back in time very far.

It all looks very much like playing with the days as we go on and off daylight-savings-time. Or, maybe it looks more like a case of Dennis the Menace playing on December 31st, 1999, at the 180° meridian of longitude, quipped by man-made agreement as the "International Date Line." Dennis would be standing with his left foot on the west, Dec. 31, 1999, side of the line then hop onto his right foot – onto the east side which would already be January 1, 2000. "Hey, mom," he'd say with pride, "I hopped into the next

---

63 chapter 10, p.106.
64 Ibid, p.109
65 Ibid.

century!" And then with a hop back onto his left foot, "Mom, watch me go back in time!" Of course, being the little devil he's known to be, he'd really give us all a run for the money by doing jumping jacks: "This is how you can be in two different centuries at the same time!"

But then again, in all seriousness and to get back on track, all the tzaddikim (saints) since Jacob have been known for their ability to "jump the way" ("*kfitzat haderech*"). The stories of the Baal Shem Tov even note that the horses were blindfolded so they wouldn't get scared.

"Wait a minute. You mean to tell me the great rabbis all knew how to space travel?"

"The way you put it is a more modern way to term it. But, yes, you may be happy to hear that wormholes and time travel existed since biblical times, as recorded in the Torah. See, that's just it – there's nothing new under the sun. Not even what I just wrote. King Solomon said that thousands of years ago. And that was back when, when we would think there'd be all kinds of new stuff in the world. We need to think again. Once again.

"Okay, so three times the Torah-Tanach discusses real wormholes, which are called in Torah nomenclature 'kfitzat haderech', or 'skipping' or 'jumping the way'. The first was Abraham's servant Eliezer, who was acting in the service of Abraham, for the good of Isaac. The second to do *kfitzat haderech* was Jacob. And the third was Avishai Ben-Tzruya, acting for the sake of King David.[66] That is to say, wormholes and time travel occurred in the service and for the sake of the four persons of the Merkavah, the Chariot: Abraham, Isaac, Jacob, and King David.

"About Eliezer, we learn that he makes a point of saying that he came 'today'[67] because naturally, by the laws of physics, it would be impossible for him to have arrived on the same day that he

---

66 Tractate *Sanhedrin* 95a.
67 Genesis 24:42.

left.[68] Jacob, we learn[69] had a *kvitzat haderech* when he left Be'er Sheva for Charan and stopped by in Jericho and Mount Moriah. And, Avishai Ben-Tzruya saw that King David was in trouble in Philistine country, and, because it was already the eve of Shabbat and needed to save King David before Shabbat set in, the earth 'jumped' for him.[70]

"Holy spiritual masters have 'jumped the way' throughout the generations, as I noted before. We know that the Baal Shem Tov and Rashash (Rabbi Shalom Sharabi) and the Ari did so all the time; and many stories remain by their being told and retold, including the details of the circumstances and purposes of these trips.

"But, also as we've said before, time travel is also done all the time by all who recreate their personal history: Those who do go back and change all the cause and effect involved and place themselves on a new track. It's also called *tshuvah*, repentance.

"In this context, there's something else I want to mention here, because it's also part of the Central Column energy. It's the Doctrine of Retrospect. And, basically what it means is that anything that is in or relates to the present or future, or is moving towards a future time, then it is our duty to do tikkun, meaning to correct it in a positive, constructive, good manner – in short, make it kosher and right. But if, however, it is completely in the past and is over and done with, then we can use the powers of our mind and free will to make what was bad and evil and turn it into being what is good and positive – use the bad as an offset for the good.

"If someone was harmed in any way in the past and that abuse is still going on now, then retrospect does not apply. You cannot just say, it's okay to suffer, because it's all for the best. NO. Absolutely

---

68 Tractate *Sanhedrin* 95a and Rashi on the words *"VaEvo Hayom"* that they mean that "Today I left and today I came, indicating that jumped for him the earth."

69 Tractate *Chulin* 91b and Rashi on Genesis 28: 11

70 *Me'am Lo'ez* on Samuel 2 21: 17.

not. If an evil is still doing harm, that harm must actively be dealt with and corrected to be made right. But, if someone was being abusive, but the one abusing died and the abuse itself ended completely, then, to heal the abused and the situation, we need to use the Doctrine of Retrospect. In this last example, we would say that for whatever reason that abuse occurred, now that it's over, it must be for the best. And then we can use that negative experience as a lesson on what not to do and use the traits, strengths, and tools we've acquired in the process for the present and future. And, in this sense, we've then rewritten history."

"Cool."

"Right. But, my friend, that is only one of the navigational tools I'd like you to take away."

"Navigation? What do you mean? What am I supposed to be navigating, and where?"

"Why, navigating in the journey which is your life."

"Oh."

"You have heard, I hope, that this world is compared to a very narrow bridge."[71]

"Yeah."

"And you know that God Himself tells us that He's put before us the choice of either life and good or death and bad,[72] right?"

"Okay."

"Well, God tells us that between this choice of 'blessing' or 'curse' that we should 'choose life'.[73] And not only that, but God provides by His Book the very means of attaining the blessing, life, and good. In it, He provides you with all the navigational tools you need to successfully journey across the narrow bridge. And this is the very spiritual GPS you need for your journey and which promises success."

---

71 *Likutei Moharan* (The Writings of Rebbe Nachman of Breslev), part 2, section 48.

72 Deuteronomy 30: 16.

73 Ibid, verse 19.

"It tells me when to turn right or left, like a real GPS?" He tried to insert sarcasm.

"Actually, it's a lot better than a regular GPS. And what's more, as a general rule of thumb, God's GPS always has you go straight – it keeps you on a direct path down the straight and narrow. In fact, it's UP the straight and narrow, not down; but the path over the bridge is very narrow. So, the general rule is to never go right or left as you head toward the Promised Land[74], a term which I want to teach you as well – it's both actual and spiritually-figurative."

"The Promised Land."

"Exactly. It's a real place – the Land of Israel. But it's also part of the nomenclature of the journey."

"Sounds like a code that needs a key to decipher it."

"Well, in essence, that's the way God's Book, the Torah, is written. And, as in our spiritual GPS, the Torah, we reiterate and review the terms and directions all the time, throughout the day and throughout the calendar year. Throughout the day we remind ourselves of the direction of our individual and collective journey when we say the Shma – during the Shacharit and Maariv prayer services, Kriat Shma al-ha-mita at bedtime, and even in the birkat hamazon, the blessing after meals. That is, we remember the exodus from Egypt, because it was the root of all our subsequent exiles, just as our exodus from Egypt is the root of all subsequent and even future exoduses and redemptions.[75]

"But, now to provide you with the essential spiritual navigational tools. Basically, the same concepts and nomenclature are used in two frameworks. In the first framework[76], you learn that there are 5 stages that one must undergo in order to 'leave Egypt' – itself being a term. But see, this entails more than just a geographical change. Rather, it means releasing oneself from

---

74 Numbers 20: 17.

75 Rabbi Moshe Chaim Armoni's *Bati LeArmoni*, vol 2, *parashat 'Shmot'*, page 1.

76 From Rabbi Daniel Stavsky HaCohen shlit"a's "Guide to Exodus From Egypt: According to the PaRDeS" by the Sulam Raphael Center, 1996.

those obstacles and limitations (literally 'MaiTzaRim' – straits –
from the same root as Egypt – 'MiTzRayiM') towards a different
level of consciousness. And it's the Torah that provides the terms
and defines these stages with names that describe human mental
states.

"The nomenclature or stages are: Egypt (a state of slavery
and dependency, lack of choice), the Splitting of 'Yam Suf, which
literally means the Sea of End (where a desire awakens to leave
and disconnect ourselves from the forces that limit us and keep us
from connecting to the Endless, to God), Desert (an intermediate
stage of trials of our true desire where we already have a choice,
every moment, between going back and progressing forward,
but we are vulnerable and not yet accustomed to freedom),
Mount Sinai (where we receive the Torah, raising the mortal
mind to receive the superhuman, objective body of Law on
the workings and structure of creation, and where we acquire
mental freedom and conscious understanding of the purpose of
each action and element in this system by connecting the root
or 'head' that operates the world, the latter being the body'), the
Holy Land (where the conscious plan, received in the last stage,
is implemented – the physical place where we realize all of the
knowledge and experience accumulated in the previous stages and
where we are free to choose to act as partners of the Creator and
apply His desire, which is called the 'correction' of His creation –
the totality of which is called redemption).

"Then, once we know what the stages are and what to expect,
we then undertake the necessary preparations for the journey. For
this we make order (literally 'seder' and thus what we actually do
on the Eve of Passover) of our lives, which, just like for Passover,
first requires a thorough housecleaning (literally-physically
and figuratively-spiritually and internally) to rid all 'chametz'
(leavened-inflated traits) from our environment and from within.
Then, the 15 'simanim' that we undertake on the Passover 'Seder'
are the 15 signposts or directional markings that help us on our

journey and that also mark our progress.

"The second framework of essential spiritual navigational tools is based on the writings of the Ari[77], whereby Joseph's descent into Egypt is likened to the human body: the soul descends to this world, the latter being the 'Land of Egypt'. The key to spiritual 'navigation' (to use my term) is where the smallest passage lies – the straits (M-Tz-R-M) which is Egypt (M-Tz-R-M) itself. It is this narrow passage that is between the head and the body – i.e. the throat – through which the three channels run that determine human existence, literally-physically, and figuratively-spiritually: the trachea or windpipe, the esophagus or foodpipe, and the jugular vein.

"These three essential channels are personified by the three head ministers of Pharaoh, namely the Chief of Butlers (Sar HaMashkim) – is the trachea, the Chief of Bakers (Sar HaOfim) – is the esophagus, and the Chief of Guards (Sar HaTabachim) – is the jugular vein. And the acronym of these three ministers – Tabachim, Mashkim, Ofim, being TME in Hebrew denotes tameh, impurity. Thus, these 3 are the essence of impurity.

"The evil inclination within us pulls us away from the spiritual by overwhelming and overtaxing our time with regard to food and drink – the minister of food and drink, or 'Chief of Bakers'. The more spiritual a person is, the less he or she invests, time-wise and indulgence-wise, in eating and drinking. The epitome was Moses, who did not eat or drink for 40 days atop Mount Sinai.

"Interestingly, our entire exile to Egypt evolved from and revolved around dreams – Joseph's, the three ministers' to Pharaoh, and Pharaoh's himself. And it is through the imagery of all these dreams that God maps out the direction we should take to 'get out of bondage', plus guides us for the journey itself. This is God's GPS for our journey from low consciousness ('mochin dekatnut') to elevated consciousness ('mochin degadlut').

---

77 *Likutei Torah, parashat "VaYeshev"* as quoted in Rabbi Moshe Chaim Armoni's *Bati LeArmoni*, vol 1, *parashat 'MiKetz"*, pages 249-254.

"The low level of consciousness is a prison for the soul, and thus Joseph and the 3 ministers, at the start of our 'story' or map, are first in jail. Notice that when Joseph leaves prison, he goes straight up to rule – being his destiny – even though he was still 'down' in Egypt, in exile, which is defined as the rule of the 3 ministers. When the soul grows spiritually, it also elevates beyond the physical desires of eating and drinking. And, therefore, once the Chief of Bakers is released from prison, meaning elevated, he is hanged – that desire is killed by the higher spiritual consciousness level.

"But the Chief of Butlers is another story. His dream recounts that:

> And on the vine were 3 shoots;
> and it was as though it budded,
> shot forth its blossoms, and on the
> cluster the grapes became ripe

(Genesis 40: 10).

The 3 'shoots' are our 3 forefathers, from which came and includes our entire nation, the latter being the 'ripening grapes'; and, thus, 'a vine out of Egypt' (Psalms 80: 9).

"So, the Chief of Butlers says, 'And I took the grapes and squeezed them into Pharaoh's cup' (Genesis 40: 11). This is the upcoming bondage[78] and oppression. But, this minister is then set free to live, because that is the outcome of the Nation of Israel. After the collective test comes the unprecedented collective spiritual ascent, which also goes to unprecedented heights.

---

78 This decree was already set. The prophecy of the Covenant between the "Pieces" (*Bein HaBetarim*) is the same prophecy that foretells the Egyptian exile (Genesis 15: 9-10, 13). See Rabbi Aryeh Carmell's translation of Rabbi Eliyahu Dessler's *Michtav MeEliyahu* in the former's *Strive For Truth*, vol. 5, *parashat MiKetz*, page 172: "The first occasion when the descendants of Avraham are called 'stars' is in the prophecy of the Covenant between the Pieces, the same prophecy that foretells the Egyptian exile."

"And this is where we tie in the importance and urgency for all of Am Yisrael, the Nation of Israel, to come home to the Land of Israel. The Diaspora for us is only meant to be a temporary resting spot. There are 3 words used to describe our stay in Egypt, and they show a progression in our mindset and perception of the very meaning of our being in Egypt. The 3 verbs are: LaGur (to live), where we first perceived a temporary rental-like living arrangement; then VaYeshev (to sit), which is like buying a house just to get out of renting, but with the intention of selling it once the time is up and there's the need to move on. And the third verb is VaYechazu (and they gripped), denoting putting down roots.[79]

"History sure repeats itself. Isn't the third verb where a lot of us are holding now too? We've got it all wrong, distorted, and we need to move on. Notice exactly what it is that Moses requests of Pharaoh: **Let my people go so they can serve Me[God]**.[80] That is, the request and its purpose – to serve God. It's not just to be set free to roam without a goal.

"The path to higher spirituality is the path the Nation of Israel used to break out of the bondage of Egypt – and that path is 'messirut nefesh' meaning total devotion to Torah and to the mitzvoth, the commandments.[81] Notice the formula: 'Let my people go, and we will serve God. And, within this path is the purpose and aim of any and all spiritual exoduses – redemptions – which is: to reveal and know God. And 'knowing' is when we internalize and join our brain with our heart – our cognitive thought with our instinctual feelings.[82]

"Oh, and by the way, in this framework, the splitting of the Red Sea – or more literally: The Sea of End – has a different meaning. Dry land denotes what is revealed in this world, while the sea equates with what is hidden. So, turning the sea into dry

79 Rabbi Moshe Chaim Armoni's *Bati LeArmoni*, vol 2, *parashat 'VaEra'*, page 40.
80 Exodus 4: 23, 7: 16, 7: 26, 8: 16, 9: 1, 9: 13, 10: 3.
81 Rabbi Moshe Chaim Armoni's *Bati LeArmoni*, vol 2, *parashat 'Bo'*, page 90.
82 Ibid, *parashat "VaEra"*, page 39.

land means bringing down all the dividers and veils between what is hidden (the sea) and what is revealed (dry land)."[83]

"Like something that's concealed under the surface, under the water."

"Exactly. So, the meaning of the splitting of the sea is splitting, or cracking open what is hidden in order to reveal God's unity in the world. And it's this revelation of God's working in the world that, then, actualizes our consciousness to be able to see.[84]

"You know, the word for 'world' is 'olam', which comes from the root he'elem, meaning concealment. See, God made this world with just enough disclosure, through His concealment, to enable us free will and choice. You'll also notice that under all bodies of water, no matter how wide or deep, underneath it all is land."

"True."

"And notice that in creating this world, God says, 'Let the waters under the heavens be gathered together unto ONE place, and let dry land appear' (Genesis 1:9). God's unity, His being One, is left concealed. That's why revealing God's unity in the physical world is the spiritual job of each and every one of us, and why we all need to dive into the deep waters, sort to speak, in order to find Him."[85]

"Wait. So, did all of those historical events actually happen then?"

"Of course. In a parallel and simultaneous reality they took place in the physical world. But don't forget, God created time, and He created the Torah a thousand generations before our world even existed. It's just that we humans look to uncover the reasons and meanings of things in retrospect, whereas God worked the other way around: He created His meaning, reasons and plan and then created creation to fit the mold that He set. He created the

---

83 Ibid, *parashat* "*Yitro*", page 124.

84 Rabbi Moshe Chaim Armoni's *Bati LeArmoni*, vol 2, *parashat* 'B'Shelach", page 100-101.

85 Ibid.

events to serve the meaning that He already gave before the events happened.

"But, to sum up and present this particular piece of the puzzle in a unified, comprehensive, and comprehensible manner, we can say that, of course Egypt is a place. On the basic literal level, Egypt and the slavery therein refer to an actual, physical, geographical location and an actual, physical, historical era. Then, simultaneously, on a deeper, spiritual level, Egypt denotes the ever-present struggle within each and every one of our human souls. Plus, ultimately, on the most macro and metaphysical level, Egypt denotes This World, our physical world, as opposed to the Promised Holy Land, which denotes The World to Come."

*

"You know, with all the harsh stuff going on in the world today, what strategy do you recommend?"

"For all the terror and tell-tale signs of 'ikveta deMeshicha', the era of the Messiah?"

"Yeah."

"Well, bear in mind that whatever physical defense method you assume, the forces of evil will always spring just one more up ahead of you. So, you'll always be reacting to their new methods. If you want to be proactive in a manner – or THE manner – that's all-inclusive and pre-emptive, then the only solution is spiritual protection. The spiritual is stronger than the physical and it's the root of it too.

"Rabbi Shimon Bar Yochai in his *Zohar* noted all this. He wrote, 'Woe to those who happen to be at this time.'[86] But then he also provides the key to your spiritual azimuth and bearing."

"Okay. And that is?"

"Faith."

---

86 *Zohar* II, section 7b or per *parashat "Shmot"*, sections 96-97, and as quoted in Rabbi Moshe Chaim Armoni's *Bati LeArmoni*, vol 2, *parashat 'B'Shelach"*, page 98.

"That's it?"

"'It'?! That's everything. Rabbi Shimon writes that at the time of the Geula, God will look to see who is standing among Am Yisrael. Many unfortunately will die and others will leave to stand with the Gentiles. But those still standing on the side of Am Yisrael will be so because they 'exist at that time from faith' – in those words of the *Zohar*: '*yitkayem...be'emuna*'[87]. People overuse the phrase to keep the faith, but that is in fact the very key to survival, physical and spiritual."

*

"Then I have another question for you."

"Shoot."

"Just when is all that supposed to happen? Why isn't it happening yet?"

"Oh, my friend, the million-dollar question. We've been asking that for centuries – actually millennia."

"So does anyone offer any reasons?"

"Of course. And what's more, it's part of the discussion we just had. It's all in the Torah-Tanach. You just need the key, being the Oral Torah. But what's more important is applying what you decipher to activate your spiritual GPS. You need to actually DO it.

"So, King Saul asks his son Yehonatan, 'Why hasn't Ben-Yishai come both yesterday and today to the repast?'[88] He's asking about Ben-Yishai, get it?! See, King Saul's inquiry is really the ultimate question. What he's really asking is: Why hasn't Ben-Yishai, meaning the Mashiach!, come yet?[89]

"Okay? But, there's an answer too. And the answer actually comes far before Kings Saul and David. That's the way God works

---

87 Ibid *Zohar*, section 97.

88 Samuel 1 20:27

89 Rabbi Moshe Chaim Armoni's *Bati LeArmoni*, vol 2, *parashat 'Shmot"*, page 32.

– He created the plan and the solution before everything even started to unfurl. So, back in parashat Shmot, back when we were still slaves in Egypt:

> 'The taskmasters of Pharoah [over Bnei Yisrael] said: "Wherefore have you not fulfilled your task [literally: your law] in making brick [literally: in purifying by fire] as heretofore, both yesterday and today?"[90]'"

"Wow, it even has parallel language too."

"Exactly. So. Do you get it? **The answer**, in question form, is: Am Yisrael, why are you not fulfilling your Law, in observing Torah and the Mitzvot, which does '*libun*' and purifies your soul – **because the coming of Mashiach is dependent on this![91]**

*

"And, if you really want to know, I'll spill the beans. Exile is also directly connected with the destruction of the Holy Temple in Jerusalem – that is, the reasons for the two on the root, spiritual level.

"First of all, our Sages tell us that 'Every generation in which the Beit HaMikdash [Temple] is not built, takes upon itself as if it too [that generation] destroyed it.'[92] Secondly, our exile was actually established as an 'option' when Adam was expelled from the Garden of Eden, and the option was taken up on and 'chosen' by Abraham when he made the covenant with Avimelech. After the 'Covenant of the Pieces', the *Brit Ben HaBetarim*, exile was inevitable.

"Notice that when God asks Adam, 'Ayekah?' [Where are you?][93] that Ayekah has the same letters (in Hebrew) as 'Eichah' [Lamentations], as in the scroll written by Jeremiah the Prophet

---

90 Shmot/Exodus 5: 14.
91 *Bati LeArmoni*, ibid.
92 Yerushalmi, Tractate *Yoma* 1.
93 Genesis 3: 9.

on the destruction of the First Temple."[94]

"Yes, it's a straight-away identifiably unique word usage in both cases."

"Right. And in both cases it's the same letters and thus the same root. But to Adam it was put as a question, like asking if he wants to take that option or not. So, basically, in asking Adam, God was offering it as a potential possibility, not as a set fact like in Lamentations. But in offering it as an option, God was also hinting at the destruction of the Temple and of the exile, nevertheless."[95]

---

94 Rabbi Moshe Chaim Armoni's *Bati LeArmoni*, vol 1, *parashat 'VaYigash"*, pages 258-259.
95 Ibid.

CHAPTER 17

D an Shimon somehow contacted Jeff Sykes,[96] from the long-standing Jeff Sykes radio talk show he was on thirty years ago. He wanted to go back, and he wanted to go back on. Who knows, in a small rural midwest town, chances are it'll be the same audience, but just a bit grayer. They might even remember him. Nothing really changes. All three of us would be at the studio for the program to begin at 9:00 pm.

Dan Shimon stood aside and to himself. Most of his preparation was spent venting his concerns upward and asking for assistance for what's ahead.

Moments before the light went on, signaling the beginning of the show, I waved slightly to Dan Shimon to get his attention. He looked over at me and I slowly mouthed the words: "This time, 'Before the blind, don't place an obstacle.'" He nodded solemnly. What was wronged, this time would be corrected.

Maybe they even kept transcripts of shows that far back. Sykes opened by asking the same opening question he did last time. "Tell me, Dan Shimon, is there anything illegal about flying a small plane like yours and giving the public rides?"

"No," Donald answered tersely. "My plane undergoes the required inspections, and I'm a licensed pilot. The public is invited to come fly. And I'll be happy to show off my pilot's certificate and

---

96 Richard Bach's *Illusions*, chapter 17.

aircraft docs." Who cares how he got them or from whom – it was a good answer.

A young mother got on next and asked about the prospect of children flying with Dan Shimon. The next caller was an older man. "I remember you," he said in a gruff voice breathing heavily into the receiver. We waited for him to go on. "I thought I blew you away years ago." Another heavy silence. I could sense the adrenaline kick in in all of us.

Dan Shimon then smiled and leaned slightly forward in his chair, pleased to accept the challenge. He must have also recognized the voice. "Well, I'm back," he announced.

"You want to tell me what this is?!" the man demanded. Things obviously didn't make sense.

"Yes, I remember that you were the one who preached to me on the air," Dan Shimon began carefully. "How are you?" Silence. "I'm glad you called." He paused. "Since it was you who moralized, I'm gonna tell you that you made primarily two basic mistakes when you paid that visit with your shotgun." We could hear the caller's breathing get heavier. He was spooked, as if he were talking with a ghost. And an eerily calm and level-headed ghost now too.

"You preached to me back then as if you were so religious and moral," Dan Shimon began softly, but then surprised us all when he suddenly beefed up his tone. "Who do you think you are, mister, taking The Law – the Creator's Law and authority – in your own hands?! Didn't anybody teach you the basics which include the Commandment not to murder?!" Dan Shimon paused to let the affect intensify.

He went back to a calm brotherly voice, "It's His creation, buddy. And He already has an awesome and perfect system of law and order."

Sykes cut in and reminded Dan Shimon that back then he was saying that we're all free to do whatever we want to do, and do what's fun and makes us happy and the like.

"We are," Dan Shimon replied, though this time he didn't stop, but went immediately to qualify his statement. "But you pay a price when you abuse your right of free will. It's your free will right to choose between illusion and reality and good and evil. But it's a winner's game this world is and it's you who lose if you choose wrong." Dan Shimon was beginning to live up to his title.

"And this brings me to the second basic mistake you made," he went on. "Evil is anything that distances an individual and the world from the Creator. There's a goal of creation, and you caused yourself to get farther from your personal purpose in this world, as you also caused the whole world to be set back too." Dan Shimon said that last part in a tone as if he were actually saying, 'You're a bad boy.'

"Do you know what it means when a guy like you takes his shot gun to someone?" This time Dan Shimon had the tables turned around. "It means you're caught in the illusion this world sets up. You fell for the lie that no one's watching you. You deny the truth that the Creator is right here right now with me and with you. You obviously would not have done such a tremendously embarrassing mistake right in front of the Creator Himself had you properly internalized the fact that He was right there watching you, now would you?"

There was a click and then a dead line tone for a split second before the station technician quickly switched the line. That guy with the shotgun could have just had a heart attack for all we knew.

In fact, anyone who was really conscious of what was going on here, aside from the dialogue, would have been absolutely, totally dumbfounded, to put it lightly. It would be to witness the impossible and unexplainable taking place this very moment on Jeff Sykes' program. Too weird to fathom as real. But here it was.

The whole wonder seemed to fly right over the rest of the audience, maybe because most were only born after or too young at the time of the last airing. Others were probably just too confused, trying to figure out what was happening. And since it wasn't making any sense, they just let it go. The rest of his callers didn't even mention the flying and took him on a totally different turn – the one he truly wanted.

The call-director line lit up on Sykes' desk. "This is the Jeff Sykes show," Sykes quickly reintroduced, "and we're here this evening with Mr. Dan Shimon, the airplane flier. We have another caller. Go ahead."

"Yes. I'd like to say that I like what this speaker is saying. I have to be honest that I'm not up on what you were taking about from a couple years ago. But I'd like to ask, going back to what you said. What exactly is this goal of creation you mentioned?"

Dan Shimon barely even took a breath. He was already geared up and ready for this. "Awaiting us very soon," he began, "is an awesome, wonderful world. A world where everybody will perceive and feel and live with the presence of the Creator. And with this raised consciousness, we will all be happy. We'll see divinity in every object and thing. And everybody will talk to Him, because they will feel His nearness and deeply believe in Him. And, in turn, because of this, there will be no more sickness, mental or physical. We're lined up for a world without evil and wrong-doings, because who can do a wrong in front of the Creator Himself – right in front of His nose, so to speak? Everybody will know that evil only distances one from Him, and nobody will *want* to – it just won't be worth it." Pause.

"In short, we are looking forward to God's pre-planned New World Order."

A couple of lights blinked on and Sykes said we'd be taking another caller now. This time, from his voice, we could tell it was an older gentleman.

"Son, I don't know if you've looked out the window lately, but the world's in one big, cryin' mad mess. I don't know how you get to talk of all that pretty flowery stuff. You don't seem footed in reality."

"Yes," Dan Shimon began his answer, "that is precisely the facade of the illusion. I'll tell you what this world is likened to. It's likened to a big beautiful roll of fabric this guy gets. Amazingly beautiful in its pattern, texture, weave – in every way. But as a roll, it's not functional. So what does the fella do? He goes to the best seamstress he can find. The best of the best to make a gloriously-spectacular, majestically-regal robe with all kinds of fancy trimming and features, sparing nothing.

"So the seamstress says, 'Okay. Come back in three weeks and it'll be ready.' And he goes. But, curiosity killed the cat, and after only a week and a half, he's so desperately curious to see how his dream outfit is coming along, he decides to take a sneak peek, and steps by the seamstress' shop without notice.

"One peek through the window and he almost has a heart-attack *and* passes out. The big beautiful fabric is cut up into all kinds of pieces, scattered seemingly randomly all over the shop, with all kinds of loose threads and frayed pieces. How did you call it? One big cryin' mad mess. Yep, this guy sure wanted to cry alright.

"'Fool,' said the seamstress when she saw him and read the horrified expression on his face. 'I told you to come in three weeks, and you stop in at the halfway mark, pass judgment and think you can make heads or tails. If you'd just waited a bit longer, you'd see how I first tack the pieces together and then make hems and straight smooth seams to finish your robe.

'When you come when I'm done,' the seamstress continues, 'you won't see a frayed edge or loose thread anywhere in sight. Guaranteed.'

"Sir," Dan Shimon continued politely, "we're well past the halfway mark. In fact, we're almost at the end. But in a sneak preview, you still only see rough edges and an unfinished project," he finished and sat back a moment.

"Yes, you're on, go ahead," Sykes immediately got a new caller on.

"Yeah, well I wanna know how you think this planet's gonna turn into this golden gown when you've got corrupt, self-serving idiots running the show in practically every country on earth and in every field."

"They're not running the show," Dan Shimon answered tersely.

"What? I mean the heads of countries."

"I understood. They are not running the show – He is. For the most part they're all back for a second chance to make right what they messed up previously."

"And you think they're making right?"

"I'm with you – absolutely not. But the point goes deeper. This is the second and last chance they're being given by the One Who IS running the show. And that is what you need to keep in mind."

"How do you know this?"

"There's always some kind of sign. Like, back when Saddam Hussein used to sign each of the SCUDS he launched 'Nebuchadnezzar II'. He even openly declared that he was the reincarnated return of the ancient Babylonian king who destroyed the First Temple in Jerusalem.

"You'll even notice that in the original, the letters of Hussein and Sichon – the biblical king who Moses fought and defeated – the letters are the same. The Philistines and the Palestinians have the exact same letters, again in the original. In fact, their late leader Arafat has the same root letters as Orpha. Orpha was Ruth's sister who went back to her native Moab and remarried a Phillistine. She was the mother of Goliath.

"With this, you can get a mere glimpse into the real meaning of the battle between David and Goliath. David was a direct descendant of Ruth, and Goliath was a direct descendant of Orpha. David and Goliath were cousins. The battle between two polar energies that resulted from the fateful decisions of two sisters. Energies embodied and represented by two men.

"You see, history is merely the surface appearance of metaphysical forces unfolding. There are still a lot of unseen and undetectable forces pulling above and beyond what's captured on film down here. Spirituality and Torah transcend politics: They explore and explain WHY a phenomenon of any nature in any field or discipline arises in the first place, why it exists, and do not merely describe how that phenomenon looks once it has materialized on the outside.

"Ethics and morals are, then, end results – and the effects of and fringe benefits reaped from living the spiritual lifestyle of Torah. But since there is a grand master plan, we just have to let the show play out. Keep your sense of truth and justice. It's good and important."

"And on that note," Sykes cut in, "our time is almost up this evening. Mr. Dan Shimon, would you like to offer a final word to our listeners?"

"Definitely," Dan Shimon began without delay. "A practical, real and tried remedy for survival and for all that ails. Everybody in this world has his own cup of sorrow and pain. Only He can really help us, and only He really cares about each and every one of us. Talk to Him. Tell Him, in your own words, like you were taking to your dad or a friend, tell Him what's going on in your life. Thank Him for the good. This raises our virtue of appreciation and vision – our level of awareness. And ask Him for whatever you need. This is the secret of the great ones who came before us, our prophets and sages. They would find a secluded place and talk to Him with simplicity and spiritual innocence."

"Well, our time is up," Sykes cut in. "We would like to thank..."

The show was then wrapped up nicely and precisely at midnight with all the appropriate etiquette of thanking all involved. And the three of us headed back to our base. Dan Shimon looked at Aryeh Lieb, "You look pleased this time."

"This time," Aryeh Lieb explained, "they all ride off into the midnight post-sunset and all live happily ever after." They looked at each other and smiled.

"Alas," Dan Shimon chimed in, "all for one, and one for all." And the three of us laughed.

But Aryeh Lieb had his thoughts elsewhere and I saw him peek in this volume that you're reading right now, reader, as we walked.

Everything in this book is definitely true.

He closed it and handed it to me and continued to smile.

He did it.

Good.

He finished the tikkun here.

* * *

When we got back from the radio studio, Aryeh Lieb opened the volume to the part that was my journal ten years ago. I forewarned then that the Twin Towers in Manhattan would be no more, that New Orleans would be flooded, that southern Asia would too get a taste of the Great Deluge, and that the Americans and British together (TOGETHER, now who would have believed that one in 1776?) would catch Saddam Hussein and enjoy sprinkling his ashes over the sea.

He peeked at my entry thirty years ago and saw that I said that the Iron Curtain of the USSR would finally come down. It was then too unbelievable. Until these events actually occurred, nobody would have believed they would or could happen, even if we had been forewarned. He closed the book.

On a second thought, he opened the book again, this time to a page or two ahead. Next year, I will be telling people that soon Germany would undergo a tremendous earthquake and gases will rise from the ground – all the gases they used in their gas chambers when they incarnated Amalek. The next entry was that the Third Temple of Jerusalem would descend from the Heavens in fire.

"Wow!" is all he could think to say for the moment.

"Wait a minute!" he then picked up my book again. "This is not a journal, as in a chronicle. This is a schedule! No?!"

"Of course there's a schedule, Aryeh Lieb" I told him. "I told you that there's a great and wonderful plan to this world. God has in store a wonderful New World Order, just as our prophets told us all about. Isn't that what I've been trying to teach you all along?" He stopped for a moment to let the recognition set in. We were quiet. Almost instinctively, he reached for my bottle.

> *"God does not play dice."*
> *Albert Einstein*

"Tell me," Aryeh Lieb broke the silence. "So, did Dan Shimon really get murdered last time?"

"Of course. I thought you said you had a copy of Richard Bach's *Illusions*."

"And this time?"

"No. This time he doesn't get murdered. The two of you have a mission together, so he needs to stay alive."

"But if he was then..." he tried to ask, a bit confused.

"At the end of a tragedy film, does the hero die?"

"Yes."

"Right – he does. But the actor?"

"You mean the actor who plays the hero who dies?"

"Yes."

"Well, no."

"Precisely. The actor gets up, takes off his make-up and goes home. But did the hero's death effect you?"

"Ah, the vicarious reality, virtual feelings and illusions."

"Disillusions," I corrected him.

"Well, yes. I'm usually effected by virtual reality. That is, the actor really did something in the real world. And that's what counts."

"Aryeh Lieb," I tried to set things straight, "the whole world is undergoing repair. That's the framework for its schedule. Wrongs that were once done are now being corrected. You know that souls are reincarnated. And that's why."

"And there are endless lives?"

"Human – no. Everyone gets three strikes and then you're out."

"Oh."

"But that's hardly the issue," I stated. This caused Aryeh Lieb to look over at me.

"Somehow we need to stay focused, "I began, "and remember that we're all here on a mission. This is part of what gets so frustrating. There's this great plan, so tremendous and complex, it's taking six thousand years to unfold its parts to align properly. It's a great and *real* plan that involves the entire world and will be truly good to the entire world.

"And instead of perceiving this picture at large, so many insist on seeing only as far as their little cubicle. It's ugly and grotesque when you're confronted with those who refuse to even try to step a half foot outside their pettiness and vanity and see outside their little narcissistic selves.

"Because those who only see themselves are caught fast in the illusion, and are far from the reality of the whole, where – there – you can reach to the exalted spiritual level of the Golden Rule.

"So you see, there's still a lot of work to do. Don't get discouraged. Like I was saying, we need to stay focused and remember that we're all here on a mission. We all have a duty to fulfill – actually two. One, our collective one, and then each person's personal one."

"Good," Aryeh Lieb answered. "But mankind should still be entitled to a good vacation every now and then – a good movie, a day out, a day just flying."

"Maybe," I said. "I just see that most don't differentiate and see it's vacation. They're caught up in the illusion. For many, it's escape from reality. Even on daily 'doses.' Today a fancy restaurant. The next day, a show. The day after, a party. There are people that stay distracted from their very purpose here their entire lives.

"In our generation, there's constant external stimuli. Neon lights, multi-media, fast communication," Aryeh Lieb added.

"Exactly. Every day, including on vacation, people's senses are continually bombarded and over-stimulated."

"I agree," he said and then looked down to think. I gave him the extra moments of thought. He reached over to my bottle and prodded the cover to see what note would emerge.

The Fall of the Roman Empire

hypnotic non-stop commercials from Big Brother
create a desire, buy what you don't need
full-time leisurely pursuit of trivia
systematic sly swap of good and evil
arrogant, idolatrous Edom tries to lead us in singing
as if we could be the one Champion of the world
virtuous integrity compromised for entertainment
I said I loved you, but I lied
no, Jeremiah was not a bullfrog
nor Moses a cat
basic disrespect for divine values
by cheap conspicuous consumption
that'll do anything for a buck
P.S. even for their big and only – pizza
(their emperor's trademark), but
there's no more Something for Nothing
and, hey, an underdog isn't a puppy
nor 1st-degree murderers heroes
(as in the sandwich)
the great towering tree looks mean 'n lean
but its guts are rotten
and roots wasted, dude
(too stoned to know who's on first)
it'll soon all topple down
no one believed it would fall
after all, it wasn't built in a day
but when enough of us left enslavement
from behind the Iron Curtain, like Egypt
party-time got washed away
and is no more.

"The trick," I began, trying to ease back to where we were, since we hardly finished the issue, "is to be able to do whatever you do while remembering that there's a larger goal. A purpose. That all the activities we undertake for whatever purpose we assume, are only means, not the end. And remember that they're only distractions. And if you can do that, then you're free of the illusion."

"Sort of like have your cake and eat it too," Aryeh Lieb pronounced with a smile of accomplishment.

"Why not? Who says you have to be a recluse to be real? It's all a matter of where your mind is at: While you're in IT and after IT – do you realize that IT is merely a distraction?"

"Okay. What about the personal mission point? How does one know what his is in this world?"

"Well," I began, "everyone's born with certain traits. Those are your 'givens' in your formula. Negative traits are there for you to overcome. Not everyone masters that challenge, but even just working to overcome you get credit for the endeavor. It builds a person and boosts him further up the spiritual ladder." I saw that I was somewhat losing him, so decided to start from a little different angle.

"Our 'givens' are our tool box. Everyone gets a tool box. It's all a question of what and how we choose to use those tools. Here, take your plane for instance. A lot of people have or get to use planes. Some are used to drop bombs, others to dust crops, others to put out fires and others just to get people to their geographical destinations all over the world."

"Or, hey, what about hopping $3 10-minute happy spins?" Aryeh Lieb added.

"Hey, there you go."

"All the world's a stage all right. It's just a question of how one plays on his stage and how he uses his props. You might say it's also like absolute numbers. One person could be a simple [3] while another a [30]. But very definitely, a (+3) is better than a

(-30). Though, if the guy with the [30] chooses good over bad, then his [30] becomes be greater. Fame, fortune, power, genius and an infinite number of other tools are all graded by Him.

"Look in your tool box," I began, "and look in your heart. The handcuffs Houdini used in his escape feats are the same that cops use. The animals circus folk work with are the same the zoo-keepers work with. Two identical twins could have identical tools, but each would have his own energy of passion in his heart for how to use his tools."

Aryeh Lieb's head started to nod slightly and he looked pleased. "Ah, 'Fool,' said my muse. 'Look in thy heart and write!'" he said with a good attempt at an English accent.

"There you go," I acknowledged. "And you know what? I'll bet you Sir Philip Sidney himself didn't even know what he meant when he wrote that," I concluded. We smiled and nodded together.

"Problems arise when people don't live by those three parts: their general, collective purpose, their personal, individual tools, and what their heart dictates. When one is not incorporated, one feels lost and a lack of satisfaction and meaning. A person can be doing what he does quote-un-quote 'best,' but he really only refers to the tools in his tool box. If he's not using those tools in the particular way his heart 'sings,' then he won't feel satisfaction and purpose."

A silence of engrossed minds fell over our conversation. Aryeh Lieb casually leaned over and almost, as if he were just testing for fun, fingered the new note:

> *The world is too much with us;*
> *late and soon,*
> *Getting and spending,*
> *we lay waste our powers.*
> **William Wordsworth**

He raised his eyebrows in surprise. Then he slowly let go.

ONE.

CHAPTER 18

Aryeh Lieb had Spaghetti-Os and a Campbell's Soup can propped on an open fire, I guess oblivious of kashrus just yet. The good shepherd was tending them well. "What's the good word, matey?" he asked doing a fairly good Irish accent.

"Goodness. We're alive and breathing!" I don't think he even expected me to answer.

"Ah yes, my dear Watson, yet another day to learn and grow spiritually," he was obviously in a happy mood. The clean air and wide open spaces are conducive to this. Nobody's around but the crickets.

Granted, I could have reciprocated and had a good ole time. But I couldn't help myself. Remarks like that are provocative. "Who's to say we're actually growing? Advancing? Maybe we think we are but are actually fooling ourselves, when in fact we are going the other way?"

"I feel like I'm advancing. Shouldn't that be enough," he asked, still with a good cheery smile on his face.

"Do you think you can grade yourself? Or can anybody else, for that matter?" I started. "That could be another part of the illusion. It gets you to think, 'Hey, I moving up!' when in actuality, sometimes it's the polar opposite.

Just then Dan Shimon's aircraft came into view. We got to witness yet another other-worldly, slow-motion landing. It sort of caused my mind to recall those scenes from the cartoons we watched as kids: The character runs so fast, he runs a straight line off a high cliff, almost like running on an invisible plank. He stops in mid-air and, by virtue of the cartoon artist's poetic license, is afforded a good long moment to look down and eventually come to the realization that he's about to fall a long way down. At that precise moment of awareness he somehow becomes instantly capable of running back along that invisible plank, just enough to grab the edge of the cliff with his fingernails.

In all honesty, I never knew how to take those scenes. As a kid, I wasn't sure if that was intended to be funny and I was supposed to laugh or at least be impressed. Somehow I remember feeling scared for the poor critter. But what a feat – to walk on thin air.

"Wow," Aryeh Lieb exclaimed, "what a spiritual guy!" I didn't answer. Sure that I agreed, Aryeh Lieb shot an asking look at me.

"So you think his landing is a measure of his spirituality." I made it more a statement than a question.

"Mind over matter," he answered. "He's got that control."

"You've 'eaten' the illusion," I answered flatly. "A form of control you may be watching. But like meditating on a rock for hours, in truth, it's no indication of 'spirituality.'" He gave me a puzzled look. "And I'm sure you probably think that playing with clouds will earn you a magna cum laude. And then after that you could, of course, graduate summa cum laude once you're walking through walls." Aryeh Lieb shot me a loaded look, terribly annoyed to say the least.

"Let's call a spade a spade. All of that is just great self-occupation. More of ME. But what does 'spiritual' really mean?" I went on and inevitably completely ruffled his feathers.

"That's not nice," he said, straining at politesse.

"Look," I replied. "Do you want nice or do you want the truth? Remember, that's part of the test of free will and the illusion – like to be caught up in a game and think it's real, or get caught up too much in a movie and forget it's not reality. 'Truth' and 'real' are sometimes hard pills to swallow. At least at first." He was listening, but looking at me from an angle. He was consciously trying hard to swallow the first round of 'pills.' Actually, it wasn't a first round. We'd been over this before. It may have seemed then external, for others. Now it was hitting home, becoming personal.

"Once you're comfortable and happy to relinquish what's not real, you'll find that living with 'truth' and 'real' is the most uplifting form of living." I could sense he began to accept what I said, at least resolve to give it a shot.

"And by the way," I continued, "I never said he isn't spiritual. I just noted that feats per se are not a measure of spirituality. And we need to separate aspects under the subtitle 'reality' from those under 'spirituality.' It's not the same thing.

"There are so many components to what is really 'reality,' and the majority are not seen or perceived, at least to the average Joe. From micro- and radio-waves and germs to intuition, good or bad 'vibes' and personal 'chemistry.' But all this clandestine level is rendered powerless when we connect to the Creator of all things, these things included. Whether it was the witch of Ein-Dor, the sorcerers of the Pharaohs or Bilam and King Balak, those who 'walked' with the Creator overcame and thrived. Even the Amalekites, who took advantage of King Saul's fatal error of mercy and shape-shifted into sheep. They too, in their present forms, are to be completely vanquished.

"Take, for instance, the miraculous assistance Pinchas and Kaleb had in spying out Jericho. On the physical, visible level, there were the seven huge walls that surrounded the city. In addition to the sorcerers of Jericho, there were those who knew how to swear demons to surround the city and protect it from enemies. But who do you think won?"

He turned to the bottle that I brought and seemed reluctant to view the new message, but pulled it carefully anyway.

> 'Tis strange – but true;
> for truth is always strange;
> stranger than fiction
>   Lord George Gordon Byron

He let it submerge, but then tried his luck and tried for another. It would allow him a break from the conversation. Maybe he was looking for an answer to support his mixed thoughts. He took one look and somewhat jumped.

"Oh, this time it's a poem," he declared. He must not have seen the previous ones.

"Yes. That does seem to be a more appropriate form of presentation, considering your present temperament," I said softly with a half smile.

> ### Absolute Reality
> **Part I**
> *it seemed like yesterday an old*
> *garment said farewell to its generation*
> *of fashion, placed deep in a closet*
> *for the next time this fashion would repeat*
> *its turn in the cycle*
> *to be rediscovered – in its pocket*
> *an old, misplaced, forgotten picture of two children*
> *with two names on the back, one being hers*
> *so she had a brother? she had never known*
> *but here he is now – proof – right now,*
> *a displacement of then right now*
> *creating a new reality by the addition*
> *why she had not known until then*
> *shaped her reality, which is a part*
> *like a partial truth (a lie?)*
> *of the picture at large – that was small and faded*
> *but served its purpose, in its time.*

Part II

documented reported evidence
in black & white
written in the paper –
flimsy hard copy –
cut it out and filed as fact
without noting the correction posted
later
creating darkness in understanding
from white lie
how many millions read the lie?
how few read the note?
all those term papers substantiated,
prejudices evoked,
conclusions reached
all based on a mistake
all devoured without checking the ingredients.

Part III

everything known
everything obvious
and not so obvious
plus
everything unknown
yet, but will be
plus
everything unknown
and that will remain as such,
because we are limited mortals
thinking only linearly, logically
<u>not all is linear or logical</u>
Absolute Reality
the grand total

Aryeh Lieb looked up, but held a finger on the note he just read. Dan Shimon already landed and was next to Aryeh Lieb now noticing his fingers holding a new note. This got the latter's interest.

"Let's see what ya got."

> ### St. Elmo's Fire
>
> *It's always the fool who is the wise*
> *before the king*
> *it's only an illusion, the joker explains,*
> *a conscious suspension of disbelief*
> *that those alone on the cold, dark sea*
> *of life, invented to keep*
> *them going when no land was in sight*
> *(that social, controlling alternative of, life)*
> *only opaque, bottomless sea.*
> *Silly old generation*
> *today we know the sea has a bottom*
> *we've journeyed to it, have touched down*
> *to create a false god*
> *(and defy the control)*
> *that sustains their belief with false messianic light*
> *But to uncover the truth, human flesh*
> *must experience the cold, dark bottom*
> *of their journey out at sea*
> *After generations that we have masked*
> *our knowledge that the fiery Elmo the Saint*
> *is merely a trick of nature's playing magic –*
> *dulling our senses and sensibilities –*
> *before our pretending eyes*
> *that make the god eternal*
> *allowing us to be out-of-control*
> *by perpetuating the belief of meaning*
> *of our mortal lives.*

Aryeh Lieb looked up looking totally bemused. Dan Shimon seemed amused. "Oh come on," Aryeh Lieb began. "I've seen, and I'll admit it was on TV, but I saw documentaries of these guys from the Far East walking on hot coals."

"I've also seen them walk on nails," I agreed. "And I remember seeing a weird feat where this really flexible guy did some kind of yoga moves and slowly made himself into a little ball that fit in this tiny box. And he stayed in there in that position for I think an hour. So?"

"But that was real," he pleaded.

"No one is arguing if it's real or not," I said. "I just don't call that 'spiritual.' Entertainment and attention-getting, no doubt. Hey, why don't you try the next entry and see how you weather that." He looked hesitant, almost as if he were considering whether or not to accept a dare. Dan Shimon, who was still smiling, flipped the note open with his finger.

E Pluribus Unum

I celebrate not myself, nor sing myself
or at least try not, work to uproot my self,
for every atom in me belongs to Him
the Endless sea, constant transmission of life
I am merely a drop longing to return to His sea
blend with borderless oneness
egocentricity bears no fruit, tho' you may
define your self as poet
a bed-fellow like yours chops down your family tree
your breast of herbage is beneath mortal form
song must be directed, for energy is never lost
and no one lives in a vacuum
I sing to this sea, that even a leaf of grass
all stems and grows from His root,
the true origin of all poems and song
I am my soul, the other to you
material is material fact to you, that you confuse
the spirit cannot be called by just any other name
the Creator breathed living spirit into Man,
who was once the only one, but not alone

Both looked up and handed me back the bottle. Dan Shimon was still smiling and Aryeh Lieb still not. "So let me see if I understand," Aryeh Lieb began. "Being spiritual means acknowledging my place in the grand scheme of things."

"Okay," I acknowledged. "That's a good start: Perspective. What you delineated was proper perspective. Man can, at best, do a good job at a position the Creator offered him to fill. It's His show, and he can fire me from that position or give me a raise or whatever. But He's still the boss. Good. But being spiritual is a function of a couple of factors. That was just one. What about knowledge? You need to ascertain that your knowledge is like your flying with up-to-date and correct maps and charts. That's two.

"A spiritual person would naturally live by the Golden Rule, Love Your Neighbor As Yourself. And, as the greatest poet of all times envisioned and wrote... Why don't you try it again and read it yourself. Just see what pops up and read it," I said looking at my bottle in Aryeh Lieb's hand. He tugged the new note that surfaced.

> *A world of kindness and charity will be built.*
> *King David's Psalms 89: 3*

"God has in store for us a whole New World Order."

"New World Order? Is that the term? Why do I feel I've heard that before?"

"Yes. Why? Did you think I referred to the one that George Carlin described as the Big Club, the owners of the physical world who own the big corporations, the media, the governments? Well, that club of the souls of the 974 generations are powerful, but never as powerful as He who really runs the world.

"The Creator of the world lets us try to run things ourselves, but we mortals only messed up the world big time. God will appoint us a king, we will live according to Torah, and all those cameos I showed you from my special album – of the verses describing what will be – all will come into fruition. No more man making the rules and trying to rule and order the world. You thought the New World Order was some mortal, evil conspiracy? No. God rules and orders things here. And everywhere for that matter.

"The less a person is connected and caught up in this world, the more spiritual he is. A person can live and function, even work a full 9-to-5 plus a little overtime, and be involved in this world, but if he's spiritual he's not duped or interested in all the illusions and stimuli of the material world. Paradoxically, he'd work to better this world for others – the Golden Rule, to help others.

"Oh, one more thing," I continued. "This actually should have been first. It could actually be considered part of the first element.

The more one thinks of the Creator, the more spiritual he is. A true saint would be one who doesn't stop thinking of Him for even a moment. And a mere moment that he would take his mind off of Him, for the saint, that would be considered sin.

"That, of course, also says something about the rest of us. At least myself," I confessed. "I get all excited when I can focus my thoughts properly even a fraction of the day. For those moments, I feel connected. But those are only sparse moments. Typical layman."

"So what would be a great achievement for the layman would be peanuts for the truly spiritual. In this framework, it's relative. His moment of 'sin' would be a great spiritual rise for someone else."

"Right. The appearance of the world is like a mask. It's easy to forget that. There are even those whose jobs it is to sell you illusions or encourage you to remain in the daze."

"I think there are a lot of fields out there that do that. Keep you hooked." I nodded. Aryeh Lieb considered that a moment and reached for the bottle.

> *"Don't part with your illusions."*
> **Mark Twain/Samuel Clemens**

> *"It is possible to live only as long as life intoxicates us; as soon as we are sober again we see that it is all a delusion, a stupid delusion."*
> **Leo Tolstoy**

"I see that it's an on-going struggle to counter the illusion. To truly break free and overcome the illusion – that's a tough call."

"Aryeh Lieb, just say a tough challenge. And you like challenges. You're tough."

"Well, I do want to overcome the illusion. Get above and

beyond it. Live in a state where I'm connected only with what's really real."

"Hear ye, hear ye! Friends, Americans, countrymen, lend me your ears. I've come to bury the illusion, not to praise it...or to succumb to it!"

"Yeah, right," he mumbled with pursed lips then laughed.

"Well, you should know that you get credit above just for having good desires. The very fact that you make such a positive, proactive decision towards what's right and good – you'll get a 'return' on that in time."

"Nice," he said and half-smiled looking away. "Tell me," he began on second thought, "why would anybody, who understands the difference and the implications, choose the illusion?"

"Because the problem with knowing the truth is that it's obligating," I answered. "On the other hand, though," I added, "it's extremely rewarding."

"I'm with you, but I have to admit...what can I say, I like a good novel or movie every once in a while. I mean fiction. You know, the non-real."

"Hey, we all love a good story every once in a while," I agreed. "That's not the same as what I mean about illusion."

"But the fantasy isn't just entertainment. For some people, it helps numb the pain that life doles out. It's an easy and legal escape."

"So you have a double whammy. You've got the illusive facade of the physical world that gives the appearance that this is it: it's only the physical world that exists. It doesn't let you see that it's an emanation and expression of the Creator Himself. And, then, on top of that you have the fantasy illusion, created to entertain, distract and even drug us.

"It's a fine line to walk to see through all that. Not everyone succeeds. There have been people who have murdered under the influence of a fictional book or picture. And people miss out on 'live' relationships, because of misperceptions or even obsessions with fictional characters. They're caught hook, line and sinker fast in the illusion.

"On the other hand, fantasies can help enhance what is real. If you acknowledge it only as a means to an end, it can be a good aid and vehicle to get to better places.

"Fish again," I instructed pointing to my bottle.

> *Illusion and reality.*
> *The former enchanted most people these days;*
> *the latter had been out of fashion for years…*
> *humanity preferred fantasy over truth.*
> *Dean Koontz*

"Well, I'm here in part to bring reality back into fashion and to show that it's just as enchanting, if not more."

CHAPTER 19

"O kay. I choose the blessing and life. Now where do I start?"
"Awesome. Good choice. And right choice.
"The start of the journey and throughout the journey, keep to the source, the fundamentals, the essentials – the basics of it all. The Nation of Israel has 613 commandments plus its Book, THE Book.

"Actually, let me give you a 3-point program for starters, but which is really for the entire journey. First, you need to just plain read the Written Torah that God instructed Moses to write down. Start, literally, from 'In the beginning, God created the Heaven and the Earth' – from the opening words of "Bresheet bara Elokim…" in Genesis 1: 1 straight and all the way through to the final ending words "Mi bachem mikol amo Y-H-V-H Elokav imo vyaal" of Chronicles 2 36: 23.

"And, as you read the '5 Chumashim' or 'Books' of the Torah of Moses, bear in mind that in reading, you are really only familiarizing yourself with the outer, literal level; and, that to actually understand what's going on, to decode it, you'll need the Oral teachings that Moses received from God during the former's 40-day stay up on Mount Sinai – the Oral Torah. They go hand-in-hand and together are The Torah.

"To get in your regular study of the Oral Torah, you can do what many do all over the world – the *Daf Ha Yomi*, the Daily Page.

Everyone worldwide following the *Daf HaYomi* is on the same page of the Talmud and everyone finishes the entire *Gemorah* every seven and a half years. It's a wonderful, unifying thing. You read one page of Talmud a day, according to the worldwide schedule, where everyone reads the same page; and you can take a class anywhere in the world too. Do it. Sign up, get your Oral Torah in and connect with our Nation. It's great. Okay, that's One.

"Two is the basic meaning of being a Jew, of the Nation of Israel. You must have in front of you the definition and meaning of what it means to be a Jew, because the definition carries with it the meaning and purpose. The whole concept of our exodus from Egypt, what that means, and why God keeps reminding us 'I am Your God, Who took you out of the Land of Egypt, to be your God.' We've gone over most of that: The meaning of exile and exodus. But that's B in your ABC's.

"And, Three is a means of connecting with authentic Torah, by way of two classic books: *Tomer Devorah*, Deborah's Palm, by the Ramak, Rabbi Moshe Cordova; and *Messilat Yesharim*, The Track of the Upright, by the Ramchal, Rabbi Moshe Chaim Lutzato.

"Tomer Devorah will teach you how to live according to the attributes of the Ten Sefirot and the Thirteen Virtues of Higher Compassion. Note its opening.

> Man is suitable to [act] in likeness of his Maker, and then he will be [included] in the secret of the higher form, tzelem [image] and character. Whereas if he is similar in his body but not in actions, then he disappoints the likeness…Therefore it is right to [act] in likeness to the actions of the Keter (Crown), which are the 13 Virtues of Higher Compassion as hinted in the secret of the verses (Micha 7: 18-20)…

"The title of *The Book of the Track of the Upright* is taken from Mishley, Proverbs 16: 17 – 'Track of Upright, leave evil, protects one's soul, forms one's path.' This book summarizes the Components of the complete Service of God as 1. Awe, 2. Going in His Ways (Integrity of Perfecting Virtues), 3. Love of God and Gratifying Him, 4. Wholeness of Heart, that the service of God is with purity of intention, and 5. Keeping all the mitzvot, commandments, being the means of the Service.

"The root of wholeness of service – Authentic Piety – is that it should be clear and verified to a person what one's duty is in the world, and why one needs to focus and direct everything one strives for one's entire life. The means to attaining our purpose are the commandments, the mitzvot; and the place we can do them is only in this world – i.e. this world enables us to do them. The basis of the Track is that verse in Deuteronomy 10: 12,

> And now, Israel, what does Y-H-V-H your God ask of you but to [have] awe of Y-H-V-H your God, to walk in all of His ways, and to [have] love of Him and to serve Y-H-V-H your God with all of your heart and all of your soul.

And, the actual path, the 'Terms of Service' being the Track, is comprised of twelve steps or levels: Torah (1) leads to Carefulness (the mitzvoth of omission, or negative commandments), which leads to Agility (the action mitzvot, or positive commandments), then Cleanness, Abstinence, Purity (of heart and thoughts), Piety, Humility, Sin-Fearingness, Holiness, the Holy Spirit (above natural law), and Resurrection of the Dead (like Elijah and Elisha the Prophets).

*

"Well, as Alice's companion would say," I began, "'the time has come the walrus said'."

"'To talk of many things,'" Dan Shimon picked up with a laugh.

"I do think that we have talked of many things," I said. "Now it's time for me to light out for new territory."

"A new Adam?" Aryeh Lieb asked.

"Heaven forbid!" I said adamantly. "A loyal descendant of the original one." They smiled at that, but I could also see a drop of sadness in their faces, as I was finishing my last preps to get going.

"I think we've slain a couple dragons together, have we not?" I tried to raise the morale. "And, now that you've corrected your faulty parallel life, you can return home to Eretz Yisrael – reunite your body and soul. Plus, I'm delighted to remind you, now that I'm at the end of my stay and of our tale here, that, as it turns out, we're actually of nobility! Better yet, fortuitously, of royalty. Serendipity at its best: We are all His children. Each and every one of us is like an only child of the Creator, THE King of Kings.

I started to walk away.

"Now really, where are you off to?"

"Me?" I began. "I'm going back to my spiritual island.

"The uncharted new frontier, huh? Your island sounds exotic."

"No."

"Tropical?"

"No."

"So where is it?"

"It's my study at home." They looked at me surprised.

"And on that note, I guess I'll bid ye farewell for now, but not for long. Okay, Prince Aryeh Lieb? And you too, Prince Dan Shimon?" And they smiled at that as they waved.

* * *

the end
but then, also a
wonderful new beginning

* * *

www.ingramcontent.com/pod-product-compliance
Lightning Source LLC
LaVergne TN
LVHW051737080426
835511LV00018B/3108